A Guide to Preserving the Value of You[r Home]

THE HOMEOWNE[R'S]
HANDBOOK

Published by
OMD Enterprise, Inc.

Authors:	Richard Carlisle
	Barry Prentice
Senior Editor:	Richard Carlisle
Contributing Editors:	Bill Roth
	Carolyn Linville
	Jenifer Sullivan
Photo Credits:	Barry Prentice
	Jay Keany
	Richard Carlisle
	Tom Prentice
Copy Reviewers:	Janet McRoberts
	Odie Snell
	Jay Keany
	Ellen Hickernell
Cover:	Annie Kennedy
Senior Designer:	Annie Kennedy
Assistant Designers:	Sarah Yongprakit
	Chris Goodspeed

Manufactured in the United States of America

Copyright 2004, 2014 OMD Enterprise, Inc.
All Rights Reserved.
Published by OMD Enterprise, Inc.
Louisville, CO 80027

To reorder: 1-800-490-6907
www.inspectorstuff.com
ISBN: 0-9729556-0-7

The Homeowner's Handbook

Dear Homeowner,

If you have a copy of *The Homeowner's Handbook*, it probably means that you have recently purchased a house or had a home inspection. Your home inspector took a "whole-house" approach and reviewed the condition of many of the key elements in your home, including:

- Roof
- Electrical systems
- Basement or crawl space
- Foundation
- Heating/cooling system
- Walls and ceilings
- Plumbing
- Floors and windows

In short, the home inspection was a bit like a physical examination. You know the condition of your home at this point in time. But, of course, time moves on and the condition of your home can change. That is why we created *The Homeowner's Handbook*. It is meant to help you understand your changing home so you can preserve its value and prevent costly calamities.

We hope that you will use this handbook as a resource to (1) understand the basic construction of your home, (2) identify steps you can take to prevent problems, (3) develop a schedule for routine maintenance, and (4) identify equipment that can safeguard you and your home.

Home ownership is a treasured accomplishment—but it is also a big responsibility and one that you need to accept for many years. We hope this objective information will help you with that responsibility so your home can provide safety, security, and comfort for your family.

CHAPTER 1
From the Ground Up

Overview 9

**Section 1: The Foundation–
Getting to the Bottom of It All** 10

Perimeter Wall
on Spread Footing Foundations 11

Grade Beam on Caisson 12

Slab-on-Grade Foundations 13

Thoughts About Foundations 14

**Section 2: The Floor System–
What's Hiding Under The Carpet?** 15

Poured-in-Place Concrete Floors 15

Framed Floor Systems 15

"Floating" Floors 16

Finishing Basements 16

**Section 3: Walls–Supporting the Roof
and Keeping the Weather Out** 17

Bearing Walls...17

Non-Bearing Walls 17

**Section 4: The Roof–
Keeping a Lid on It All** 18

Joist and Rafter System 18

Factory-Fabricated Trusses 18

**Section 5: Soil–
Its Effect on a Home** 19

**Section 6: Exterior Moisture–
Its Effect on a Home** 20

**Section 7: Remember the Following Tips
When Evaluating Cracks and
Their Structural Symptoms** 22

Home Protection—
Looking Out for Culprits.................................23

Start by Looking at Your Home
and Ask the Following Questions...................23

Chapter Conclusion 23

CHAPTER 2
Exterior Weather Shell

Overview 25

**Section 1: Roof Coverings–
Protecting the Home Below** 26

Sloped Roofs 26

Flat or Low-Sloped Roofs 27

Extending the Life of Your Roof......................28

Roof Flashings...28

**Section 2: Wall Cladding–
Decorative and Functional** 29

Masonry Walls 29

Wood and Wood-Composite Siding................29

Stucco 29

Exterior Insulated Finish System 30

**Section 3: Garage Door Opener Safety
and Maintenance** 31

Section 4: Outside Hose Faucets 32

Conventional Hose Bibbs 32

"Freeze-proof" Hose Bibbs 32

**Section 5: Winter Shut Down
of Sprinkler Systems** 33

When and How to Shut Down
a Sprinkler System..33

Chapter Conclusion 33

The Homeowner's Handbook

CHAPTER 3
The Twists and Turns of Plumbing

Overview 35
Section 1: Aerator 36
Section 2: Washers 36
Section 3: Cartridges 37
Section 4: Toilets 38
Section 5: Disposers 39
Section 6: Water Heaters 40

Some Important Information
Regarding Water Heater Safety 41

T&P Relief Valves and Discharge Tubes 41

What Are You Storing
Around Your Water Heater 41

Chapter Conclusion 41

CHAPTER 4
Electrical Systems and Safety

Overview 43
Section 1: Overhead Wires 44
Section 2: A Lifesaver–The Ground
Fault Circuit Interrupter (GFCI) 45

Wall Receptacle 45

Circuit Breaker 46

Portable 46

Section 3: Illuminating Facts About
Home Electrical Systems 47

Answers to the Most Often Asked
Electrical Safety Questions 47

Section 4: Aluminum Wiring–
Then and Now 50

The Characteristics of Aluminum Wire 50

Resistance 50

Ductility 50

Compatibility 50

Section 5: Your Electrical Service Entrance
–Always at Your Service 51

Main Disconnect Located at the Meter 51

Main Disconnect Located
in a Multiple-Service Meter Bank 51

Main Disconnect Located in the Main
Distribution/Branch Circuit Panel 52

Split-Buss Panels 53

Securing Outside Electrical Equipment 54

Section 6: Electrical Applications
Commonly Found in Homes 54

Protected Exterior Outlets 55

Horizontal Outlets 55

3-Way Switched Lights 55

Proper Mounting of Ceiling Fans 56

Section 7: Alarms and Detectors 57

Smoke Alarms 57

Carbon Monoxide Alarms 57

Propane Gas Alarms 57

Chapter Conclusion 57

CHAPTER 5
Heating System Essentials

Overview 59
Section 1: Forced Air Systems 60
   Air Filters 60
   Installing Air Filters 61
   Humidifiers 61
Section 2: Hot Water Systems 62
**Section 3: Hot Water Heating Systems–
Maintenance Steps** 63
**Section 4: Traits of Fuel-Fired
Heating Appliances** 64
**Section 5: Radiant Ceiling
Heating Systems** 65
Chapter Conclusion 65

CHAPTER 6
Home Cooling Systems

Overview 67
**Section 1: Central Air/
Refrigerated Systems** 68
   Maintenance Tips 68
Section 2: Evaporative Coolers 69
   Maintenance Tips 69
Section 3: Whole-House Fans 70
   Maintenance Tips 70
Section 4: Ceiling Fans 71
   Maintenance Tips 71
Chapter Conclusion 71

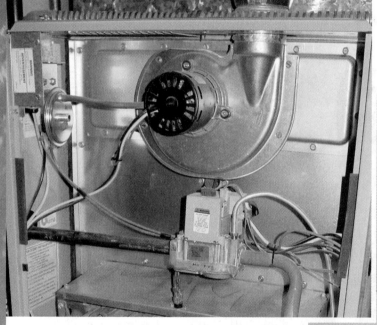

CHAPTER 7
Caring for Interior Components

Overview 73

**Section 1: Dealing with
"Signs of Maturity" in Your Home** 74

Nail Pops 74

Shrinkage Cracks 74

Doors That Rub on Their Frames 75

Squeaky Floors 75

**Section 2: Considerations for the
Laundry Area** 75

Clothes Washer Water Supply Hoses 75

Discharge Standpipe Size 76

Dryer Venting to the Exterior 76

**Section 3: Indoor Moisture
Management and Ventilation** 77

Chapter Conclusion 77

**Seasonal Home
Maintenance Checklist** 78

ENERGY SAVERS

Introduction 80

Your Home's Energy Use 81

Formulating Your Plan 81

Insulation and Weatherization 83

Insulation 84

New Construction 86

Weatherization 87

Heating and Cooling 89

Ducts 90

Heat Pumps 91

Solar Heating and Cooling 92

Fireplaces 92

Gas and Oil Heating Systems 93

Air Conditioners 93

Programmable Thermostats 94

Water Heating 95

Solar Water Heaters 96

Windows 97

Buying New Windows 98

Landscaping 99

Lighting 101

Indoor Lighting 101

Outdoor Lighting 101

Appliances 103

Dishwashers 103

Refrigerators 104

Laundry 106

Major Appliance Shopping Guide 108

Source List 110

References 112

GLOSSARY 114-119

INDEX 120-123

NOTES 124-128

IN CHAPTER 1

- How the strength of your home starts from the bottom up

- Why moisture is your home's enemy

- Why some walls support while others just "hang around"

- How many foundation problems actually start on the roof

Overview

I t is easy to fall in love with a home. Spacious rooms, a unique style, a pastoral setting—all can work their magic. A home may be the fulfillment of a dream; but a home is still a structure. This is why we are beginning "The Homeowner's Handbook" by discussing your home's main structural elements: the foundation, walls, and the roof.

Of all the chapters in this book, Chapter 1 can help save you the most money. The reason is simple: structural problems in a home are expensive. In fact, they can cost you tens of thousands of dollars in repairs! Covered in this chapter are three common types of foundations, two types of popular floor systems, and tips on finishing basements. Also included are two different types of walls along with two types of common roof systems. Most importantly, the soil under the foundation and the effects of water and moisture on the foundation are covered as well, along with tips on evaluating a foundation for potential problems.

For example, did you know that too much moisture in your attic or crawl space could crack, rot, or warp parts of your house? This chapter will give you ideas for avoiding those problems and for maintaining your home's structure. By using the information in this chapter, you can keep your home sound, your bank account healthy, and your sleep peaceful.

As with any procedure, only take on the tasks that you can safely and accurately accomplish. As always, if in doubt about anything regarding this chapter, seek the help of a qualified or licensed professional.

All Homes are Composed of Three Basic Elements:

A Foundation

A System of Supporting (Load-Bearing) and Non-Supporting (Partition) Walls

A Roof Structure

Section 1: The Foundation– Getting to the Bottom of It All

Let's start with your home's foundation—and the soil that surrounds the foundation. Buried in the ground and hidden behind finished walls, a foundation is the least visible part of your home. Chances are, however, that it required the most engineering because it supports your whole house on the load-bearing walls.

Before we continue discussing foundations, it may be helpful to understand the term "load-bearing wall." Imagine stacking two columns of blocks, three high, and connecting them on top with a wooden plank, Diagram A (below). In this simple illustration, you are building two load-bearing walls (the block columns) to support a load (the wooden plank).

In your home, the weight of the roof and the load that it carries (such as wind, rain, or snow) are supported by a system of load-bearing walls, Photo 1-01 (below). They make up the outside perimeter of your home. Load-bearing walls also appear inside your home in key areas. When a load-bearing wall is built on a strong foundation, it can support you, your furniture, appliances, and pets and still be strong enough to hold up the roof.

"A solid future begins with a solid foundation." This saying is also true for your home. In fact, the foundation is the most important part of your home's structure.

Many hours of engineering went into designing and constructing your home's foundation. Three main types of foundations are used in home construction, and your home has one of them. Just what type of foundation you have depends on factors such as (1) the weight of the home, and (2) the type of soil on which the house was built. The second factor, the soil, is especially important to a home's foundation. For example, if a home is built on soil that swells when it rains, the swelling could seriously damage the foundation and the rest of the house.

This section will help you determine your home's type of foundation and why it was chosen. At the end of this chapter, we will discuss the steps you can take to protect your home's foundation and other structural parts.

Diagram A – *Load-bearing wall*

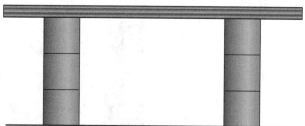

1-01 Load-bearing walls supporting the roof

Perimeter Wall on Spread Footing Foundations

Diagram B (right) shows the basic parts of a spread footing foundation. Spread (or continuous) footings are used in areas where the soils are stable, well drained, and not likely to swell because of moisture from rain or snow. The width of the footing depends on the type of soil and the weight of the home. In other words, weak soils or heavy homes mean a wider footing, Photo 1-02 (below).

During harsh winters and in colder climates, the soil often will freeze from several inches to several feet below the surface. The bottom of the frozen layer is called the "frost line." When the ground freezes, it expands and can lift or move objects. Unfortunately, this means these expanding soils could damage your home's foundation.

To avoid this problem, new building standards state that footings must be set at or below the point where the soil freezes during a normal winter. Diagram C (right) shows a footing placed below the frost line.

If your home was built between the 1920's and 1940's, it probably has a perimeter wall foundation around the entire edge of the home. In older homes, perimeter wall foundations are made with stone or brick masonry. Now, they are usually made with poured-in-place concrete. However, concrete cinderblocks, treated lumber, and even plywood sometimes are used.

Perimeter wall foundations remain popular because they allow for crawl spaces or basements under a home. Perimeter walls are also called stem wall foundations. Diagram D (right) shows a cross section of a cinderblock perimeter wall (right) and the "foundation's footprint" (left).

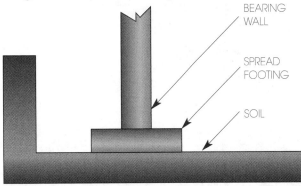

Diagram B – Spread footing foundation

BEARING WALL

SPREAD FOOTING

SOIL

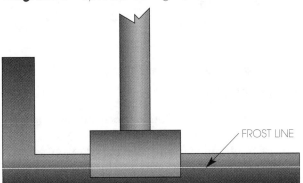

Diagram C – Spread footing set below the frost line

FROST LINE

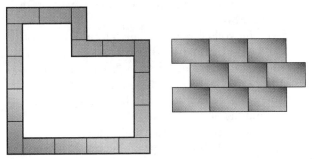

Diagram D – Perimeter wall foundation

1-02 Soil, climate, and the weight of the house dictate the type of foundation used. Shown here is a perimeter wall on spread footing.

1-03 A grade beam on caisson foundation

Grade Beam on Caisson (kaysahn)

The spread footing foundation and the perimeter wall foundation work well in stable soils. However, not all soils are stable. For example, soils that have a large amount of clay can swell when it rains or when snow melts. In fact, this soil can expand many times its original size and put a lot of pressure on a foundation. The problem is even greater if there is poor drainage away from the foundation.

Swelling soils could damage a foundation and cause a whole house to shift. In rare cases, swelling soils have made some homes so unstable that they had to be abandoned. However, even the problem of swelling soils can be managed if the right foundation is used.

One modern foundation that works well in expanding soils is called grade beam on caisson (or grade beam on drilled pier), Photo 1-03 (above). With this type of foundation, the home is sitting on solid earth and not swelling clay, Diagram E (right). The following paragraphs describe how this is done.

A grade beam on caisson foundation is started by using a truck-mounted drill rig to drill several holes into the bedrock. For most homes, a diameter of 10 inches is used. The depth of the holes can range from 5 to 25 feet or more below the foundation. The holes are drilled at each corner of the foundation "footprint" as well as about every 8 feet between the corners.

After the holes are drilled, a "cage" of reinforcing steel is placed into each hole before it is filled with ready-mixed concrete. The resulting columns are called "caissons." Photo 1-04 (right) shows the caissons shortly after they were poured.

The next step is to form and pour grade beams along the home's footprint. These beams, which

Diagram E – *Home built on caissons*

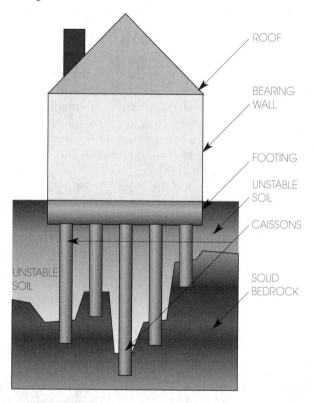

ROOF
BEARING WALL
FOOTING
UNSTABLE SOIL
CAISSONS
SOLID BEDROCK
UNSTABLE SOIL

1-04 Caissons shortly after being poured

run horizontally from caisson to caisson, are made of ready-mix concrete with reinforcing steel rods. The grade beams look a lot like the perimeter wall foundation discussed earlier, but there is an important difference. The grade beams actually transfer the weight of the home to the caissons. In turn, the caissons transfer the weight to the bedrock.

Because the beams are used in areas with unstable soil, it is important to keep them separated from the soil. To accomplish this, a specific type of material is used. This material often is made of cardboard containing air pockets that give the soil room to expand. In this way, if the soil swells, the compressible material is crushed, but the beams and the home remain intact. One such material is called SureVoid® and is shown in Photo 1-05 (below), between the soil and the bottom of the grade beam.

As noted earlier, a grade beam on caisson foundation can look much like a perimeter wall foundation. If you are unsure about what foundation type you have, consult your qualified home inspector, licensed general contractor, or engineer.

Slab-on-Grade Foundations

The term "slab on grade" simply means that a large block of concrete is poured upon the ground and serves as the home's foundation. The positive side of this type of foundation is that it is less expensive than other foundations; the negative side is that you give up the option of a crawl space or basement. With slab on grade, Photo 1-06 (below), the foundation and floor were poured at the same time. This foundation is useful in areas with milder winter climates where frost and soil expansion are unlikely to occur. It also can be a good choice for areas that have high groundwater levels.

1-06 Slab on grade with tensioning cables

1-05 Compressible void material

If the slab is to be used in areas where soil swelling is known to occur, the foundation is reinforced. Reinforcement usually means metal cables or rods are placed in a grid pattern throughout the slab. Photo 1-07 (below) shows the reinforcement materials in place and ready for the concrete pour.

Photo 1-08 (right) shows a home being built on a slab. The reinforcing cables and rods shown in this photo are inside a light blue plastic tube. The tube prevents the cables and rods from bonding to the surrounding concrete when it sets or "cures." After the concrete slab has cured, jacks will be connected to the rods that extend beyond the edge of the slab. These jacks actually pull on the rods and squeeze the concrete slab together. Because the slab is one piece, it can resist cracking when the soil below it shifts or settles. The photo also shows how the plumbing drain, waste lines, and water supply piping extend above the finished slab.

Photo 1-09 (right) shows a similar slab foundation after it was formed and poured.

Just like any foundation, a slab-on-grade foundation must support the weight of the home above. The load-bearing walls are supported utilizing one of two options. The first option is to thicken the areas of the slab to better support the load-bearing walls. As seen in Photo 1-10 (below), the thickened areas are often twice as thick as the rest of the slab.

The second option is to form and pour a separate perimeter wall. After the wall is built, the slab is poured independently inside of the foundation. Photo 1-11 (below) shows a slab-on-grade foundation where the perimeter walls are independent from the floor slab.

Thoughts About Foundations...

Understanding your home's foundation can help you preserve its strength for years to come. At the end of this chapter, we will detail more steps you can take to protect your home's foundation and other major structures.

1-08 Form work set up for a poured-in-place foundation

1-09 A slab foundation, after it has been formed and poured

1-10 The perimeter may be twice as thick as the rest of the slab

1-07 Form work and tensioning cables ready for concrete pour

1-11 Perimeter wall with the slab independent of the foundation

Section 2: The Floor System— What's Hiding Under The Carpet?

Between the foundation and the carpet, tile, or finished wood that you walk on, there is a floor system. Floor systems come in two general categories: (1) poured-in-place concrete floors (similar to a slab), and (2) floors framed from wood products (such as dimensional lumber or supported by floor trusses). Many homes have both categories, so let's explore further.

Poured-in-Place Concrete Floors

Poured-in-place concrete floors are similar to slab-on-grade foundations. With both methods, the concrete is poured directly on top of compacted gravel or soil. In buildings that have multiple floors, the concrete is poured over some type of reinforcing material. Such materials could include wooden forms or metal "pans," with reinforcing rods and cables.

Many of the home's utilities must be installed beneath the slab before it is poured. Specifically, plumbing drains, waste lines, water pipes, electrical wiring, heating and air conditioning ducts, and other services must be in place.

However, once laid, concrete floors provide a smooth surface for application of floor finishes.

Framed Floor Systems

Most homes have a framed wood floor system. Traditionally, a floor system was made from 2-inch by 8-inch (or 2-inch by 10-inch) wood boards, also known as "dimensional lumber." Wood I-joists or floor trusses also could be used. This floor sys-

tem, in turn, supported a subfloor made of plywood or oriented strand board (commonly known as OSB). On top of the subfloor, you would have a finished wood floor, tile, carpet, or so on.

Again, time and materials have changed. Now, the floor system often uses laminates of different woods. This is called "engineered lumber." Engineered lumber weighs less than regular lumber and can be installed more quickly. Factory-fabricated trusses also are available, and are being used more and more. Photo 1-12 (below) shows a framed wood floor system using I-joists. Diagram F (right) shows an I-joist.

Photo 1-13 (below) shows the underside of a floor built on fabricated floor trusses. Notice the spaces between the trusses. These spaces allow room for the placement of ducts, electrical wiring, and pipes.

Diagram F — *Wood I-beam joist*

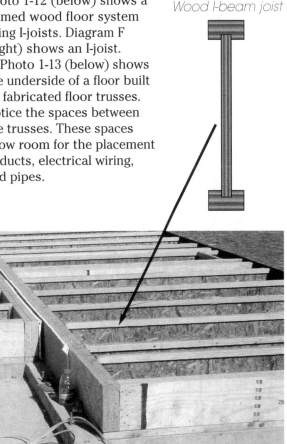

1-12 Framed wood floor system, using I-joists

1-13 The underside of a floor built on fabricated floor trusses

"Floating" Floors

Historically, basement floors were made by pouring concrete over the soil left exposed after digging the basement. With this method, the basement floor and the basement walls were all connected. In some cases, swelling soil would push up against the bottom of these floors. This resulted in humps in the floor, cracks in interior walls above, and warped door frames.

Today, "floating" has become the solution to swelling soils under the basement floor. A floated floor simply means that the basement floor and the basement walls are independent of each other. The basement walls actually hang from the floor above. Between the basement walls and the basement floor there is a gap of about 1 to 2 inches, Photo 1-14a (below). This space allows the floor to float if soils swell. The walls and the home above are not damaged by the floating floor.

Photo 1-14b (below) shows how even the basement stairs can be floated. Just like the basement walls, the stairs hang from the floor above. The only contact with the basement floor is at the very bottom of the stairs. The point where the stairs meet the landing is hinged, allowing the staircase to adjust itself if the basement floor rises.

Finishing Basements

Planning to finish the basement in your home? Before starting, you will need to check the key structural components. This means knowing what type of soil is under your basement, what type of foundation you have, and the type of floor system that was used. Fortunately, these things often are easy to determine.

First, find out if the basement floor is a wood system or is concrete poured on grade. Next, you need to determine if soil swelling is a concern. A floating staircase in the basement is a good sign that the builder expected the soil to swell. Another sign would be the presence of compressible material under the bottom of any perimeter foundation wall. Check crawl spaces if your basement foundation wall is not exposed. If you have a poured-in-place concrete floor, further questions should be asked about the soil below.

If there is any chance that the soil could swell, then any new walls should be floated. As discussed earlier, it is important for the walls and the floor to be independent of each other. This way, if the soil under the basement floor rises, the floor can rise without cracking the walls and damaging the home above.

1-14a Floating wall hung from the floor above (note support strap and gap at bottom)

1-14b Hinging at the landing above (arrow) allows the staircase to adjust if the basement floor rises

The Homeowner's Handbook

Section 3: Walls–Supporting the Roof and Keeping the Weather Out

Walls are divided into two types: bearing walls and non-bearing walls. Non-bearing walls are also called partition walls.

1-15 Bearing walls support the roof

Bearing Walls

As discussed in the "Overview," bearing walls carry the load (weight) of the home. Most exterior walls on homes are bearing walls because they support the roof above them, as shown in Photo 1-15 (above). Some interior walls also may be bearing walls if they support floors or part of the roof.

If you have an older home, your bearing walls may have been built with brick, stone masonry, or lumber. Today, if a bearing wall is made of masonry material, it is likely to be cinderblocks. Brick is still popular on exterior walls; however, today the brick is more likely to be used as a veneer rather than as a structural component.

Lumber-framed bearing walls are still popular today and commonly use 2-inch by 4-inch or 2-inch by 6-inch boards. However, other options exist. Some home builders now use finger-jointed studs, Photo 1-16 (right). Finger-jointed studs are made through a process where shorter lengths of wood are glued together and cured into longer lengths. Finger-jointed studs have the same, or greater, strength as traditional lumber.

A third option for building bearing walls is called "post and beam." Post and beam framing is popular for its ability to allow large areas of glass walls and can provide an open feeling to a living space by allowing expansive ceilings.

1-16 Finger jointed studs

Non-Bearing Walls

A non-bearing wall means just that: a wall that does not bear or carry a structural weight, Photo 1-17 (right). It simply acts as a divider or screen to provide privacy or to keep out the weather. Non-bearing walls can be framed with lumber or built of brick, block, steel studs, or stone masonry. Floating walls also fall into the category of non-bearing walls.

1-17 Non-load bearing wall (note that it does not support the ceiling)

Section 4:
The Roof–Keeping a Lid on It All

Roof structures come in two general categories: (1) joist and rafter systems, and (2) factory-fabricated trusses.

Joist and Rafter System

Diagram G (right) shows the first type of roof structure ever used by humans. This is a primitive form of a joist and rafter system.

With a joist and rafter roof, the joists are laid horizontally to provide protection from weather. The joists span from bearing wall to bearing wall. In primitive times, these roofs were flat. However, as humans evolved and mastered geometry, they learned that the triangle was one of the strongest, most efficient shapes for supporting a load, Diagram H (right). A peaked roof was made by raising the joists. Rafters were then added to provide the slope and it became known as the "joist and rafter system," Photo 1-18 (right). The result was not only a strong roof, but also one that helps shed water, snow, etc.

Joist and rafter roofs are still used in many homes that feature distinctive architecture. This type of roof can be used to create cathedral or vaulted ceilings.

Factory-Fabricated Trusses

Not all homeowners want or can afford elaborate architecture. So, many homes are mass-produced and include factory-made materials. One of those materials is the factory-fabricated truss. These trusses are made by joining individual pieces of lumber by sheet metal truss plates. The plates contain hundreds of projecting "claws" that are pressed into the lumber by hydraulic presses. The truss plates effectively bridge each joint and transfer loads from one member to the next. The result is a strong structural element. Photo 1-19 (right) shows manufactured roof trusses in use. Notice the "truss-packs" sitting on the ground waiting to be installed.

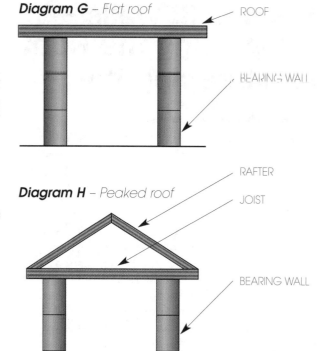

Diagram G – Flat roof

ROOF

BEARING WALL

Diagram H – Peaked roof

RAFTER

JOIST

BEARING WALL

1-18 Joist and rafter roof structure

1-19 Pre-fabricated roof trusses in use

Section 5: Soil—Its Effect on a Home

As we have stated throughout this chapter, the soil around and below your home can have a major effect on your foundation. Let's look at how the major "soil culprits" (landslide, swelling, shrinking, and settling) can affect your home.

If your home was built on a hillside, more than likely "cut and fill" techniques were used to build a perch for its foundation, Diagram I (right). Cut and fill refers to the process of cutting out the soil from the hill to form part of the platform. Unfortunately, this process could possibly cause a landslide.

Usually, the "cut" portion of the site is very stable, and a home built in this area will not settle. However, the "fill" portion of the site can be quite another story. Because the soil was cut out and moved, it does not compact as it did before excavation. The soil must be manually compacted or else, when it becomes wet, it will settle. In extreme cases, it can slide down the slope.

For these reasons, homes built on cut and fill sites should be monitored, especially during long periods of wet weather. Look for symptoms of settlement over the fill portion of the site. These symptoms might show as vertical cracking in your basement or crawl space walls.

Another issue covered elsewhere in this chapter is swelling soil. Swelling soil can push up concrete, landscaping, and even home foundations. These problems can be avoided with proper design and effective moisture management.

The last, and more common culprit, is soil shrinkage or settlement. This usually occurs where soil has been added or filled, such as around the foundation, Diagram J (right), under driveways and walkways, or in the fill portion of a cut and fill home site. Heavy rainfall, snowmelt, or poor water drainage around the foundation can saturate the soil and cause settlement.

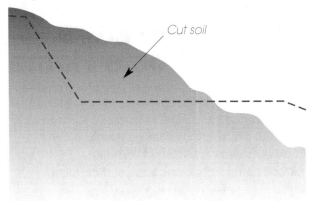

Diagram I – Cut and fill site

Cut soil

Soil is cut and filled

Stable soil "platform"

Unstable filled soil

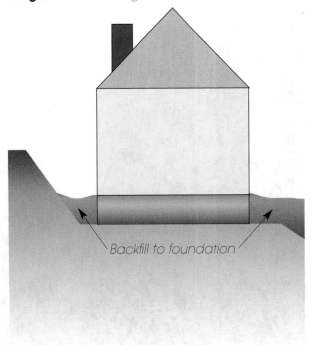

Diagram J – Shrinkage or settlement

Backfill to foundation

Section 6: Exterior Moisture— Its Effect on a Home

One important step you can take to prevent foundation damage is to monitor for signs of water in and around your home's structure. Too much moisture can seriously damage your home in several ways, including the following:

- Wood could soften, warp, rot, and even fail.

- The foundation could shift, heave, or settle. This can result in cracked walls, sloping floors, or doors that stick or fail to close.

- Pipes, ductwork, and other equipment could corrode.

- The effectiveness of insulation is reduced.

- Sidewalks and driveways could heave or settle. People could be injured by tripping.

- Personal items kept in a basement or crawl space could be damaged or ruined.

- Harmful molds and mildew could grow. These can cause respiratory illness in some people.

To protect your home, you need to be aware of where and how moisture becomes a problem.

The fact is, 90 percent of moisture problems start on the roof. If the water that hits the roof isn't directed away from the foundation, you could end up with water in the basement or crawl space. That is why a properly designed roof drainage system needs to be a priority in every home.

The drainage system involves gutters, scuppers, and downspouts. Together, they collect water from the roof and move it properly to the ground and away from the foundation. "Properly" is the key word. The water must be properly directed so that it does not pond near the foundation. Water from the roof, water hitting the sides of the home, and even water falling next to the home needs to be channeled away from the foundation. All downspouts should be extended or piped to a discharge well away from the vicinity of the home.

Sloping the ground surrounding the foundation is another good way to properly dispose of water. In general, 1 inch of fall for every foot of distance away from the foundation is sufficient. We recommend that at least the first 6 feet be sloped.

1-20 Swale

1-21 Swale

If your lot does not lend itself to extended slopes away from the home, a system of "swales" can be used to channel the water. Photos 1-20 (left) and 1-21 (left, below) show swales designed to keep water away from the foundations on these homes.

Other drainage systems can be buried when the home is built. These include foundation, French, and curtain drains. Photo 1-22 (right) shows a foundation drain before the backfill is placed. Gravel and rocks channel water extremely well, which is why they are being used here.

These drains channel the water to a sump cavity. The cavity is usually located in a corner of the basement or crawl space. If water collects in the sump, a sump pump can be installed to pump the water out and away from the building. The white pipe in Photo 1-23 (below) is the exterior portion of a sump pump discharge. Notice how the water is discharged well away from the foundation and not into the sewer.

Your roof, as well as your crawl space, can be a haven for moisture. It is important to ventilate both places. Gable, roof, soffit, and ridge vents all help to hold down moisture levels in the attic. Plastic sheeting, foundation vents, and forced circulation can be used to reduce moisture levels in your crawl space.

1-22 Foundation drain

1-23 Exterior portion of sump pump discharge

Section 7:
Remember the Following Tips When Evaluating Cracks and Their Structural Symptoms

- If you have cracks in your basement or crawl space walls, take note of their direction. If the cracks are small and almost vertical, then they are probably not a cause for concern. However, if they run more horizontally, we recommend consulting a structural engineer.

- Cracks in wood often are not significant if they run parallel to the grain of the wood. These cracks (called "checks") often are the result of the wood drying and shrinking. However, the closer the crack comes to going across the grain, the more serious it could be.

- Hairline cracks in wallboard, plaster or concrete basement walls are usually not a problem unless they are wide and look tapered ("V" cracks). These cracks often radiate out from the corners of window and door openings.

- Voids in concrete foundation walls usually are not serious unless they go deeper than an inch or so. Most of them are a result of inadequate compaction (vibration) of the concrete during placement. If a "rock pocket" allows water to come in from the outside, then we recommend having it filled with injected epoxy or another suitable sealant. Photo 1-24 (below) shows a rock pocket in a harmless location.

- Another feature shown in photo 1-24 (below) is a "cold joint." Cold joints often occur when there has been a substantial delay between the placement of layers of concrete. Usually, a cold joint is not a problem unless it leaks water or shows displacement.

1-24 Cold joint (middle) with rock pockets (above)

Home Protection—Looking Out for Culprits

We end Chapter 1 with a list of symptoms to look for and tips to follow to protect your home's structure. If you spot any of these symptoms, we recommend consulting a qualified home inspector or other expert and following their advice.

Start by Looking at Your Home and Ask the Following Questions

If you answer "yes" to any of the following questions, then there could be evidence of a structural problem (past, present, or in the making).

• Are there any sags in the roofline or in individual rafters?

• Has any part of your roof system cracked or been cut? Cutting out parts of a ceiling to install a whole house fan or a pull down access stair is a common and costly error.

• Do your walls have any cracks more than 1/16th inch across? If so, are they "V" shaped and tapered from closed to wide along their length?

• Do your floors slope noticeably?

• Do your doors close poorly or do they hit their frames?

• Are there moisture stains on ceilings, walls, or floors ANYWHERE IN THE HOUSE?

• Do you feel high levels of humidity under the house or in the attic?

Chapter 1 Conclusion

We hope the information in Chapter 1 has been valuable to you. Understanding your home's structure, and the threats to it, is the best way to prevent costly repairs. Remember that moisture is not a friend to your home's structure. Make sure you keep water away from the foundation and moisture out of your attic and crawl space. By taking these simple, but vital steps, you will be protecting your home—and your investment.

In Chapter 2, we will take a closer look at your home's roof and "weather shell."

IN CHAPTER 2

- Why your roof is actually the top of a shell

- Why walls are more than window dressing

- How to keep your "freeze-proof" faucet from freezing

- How to make your garage door convenient—and safe

The Homeowner's Handbook

Overview

I n Chapter 1, we took a bottom-up approach in learning about the structure that supports your home. In this chapter, we will take a top-down look at what covers that structure. This covering is called the "weather shell." From the roof down to the foundation, this shell protects your home's structure and everything in it—including you. The weather shell is composed of your roof, exterior walls, doors, windows, and components called "flashings." All of these elements help to keep the weather outside of your home.

Like your structure, there is much variety in what makes up this weather shell. This chapter will review different roof types including sloped roofs, and flat roofs. Extending the life of your roof and the importance of roof flashing will also be covered. We will explore the different types of wall claddings including masonry walls, wood and wood-composite siding, stucco, and exterior insulated finish systems (EIFS), and provide maintenance tips for each. We have already discussed the importance of keeping moisture away from your home's foundation. We will not repeat that information here. However, we have included sections about your outside hose faucets, "winterizing" sprinkler systems, and garage door safety and maintenance.

As with any procedure, only take on the tasks that you can safely and accurately accomplish. As always, if in doubt about anything regarding this chapter seek the help of a qualified or licensed professional.

The Weather Shell of Your Home Includes:

Windows and Doors

Roofing and Flashing

Exterior Walls

Section 1: Roof Coverings– Protecting the Home Below

Roof types come in two general categories: (1) sloped roofs, and (2) flat or low-sloped roofs. Let's explore these two main types and the materials that are used on each type.

Sloped Roofs

Most roofs are sloped, and many are covered with asphalt-composition shingles. In fact, this type of material is the most common roofing material, and is used on more than 80 percent of American homes. Asphalt shingles are used on roofs that have a moderate to steep slope. When the shingles are nailed in place, they resemble and function like the scales of a fish. Asphalt shingles effectively shed water down the roof. Photo 2-01 (below) shows asphalt-composition shingles.

A roof also could have wood shakes, tile, or slate. The fact remains that none of these outer materials actually protects the house and sheds the water. Instead, it is the material under the shingles, or underlayment, that keeps out the water. The real function of the wood, tile, or slate is to provide a pleasing appearance and to protect the underlayment from nature.

Wood shingles also are used on roofs with a slope. Both cedar shakes and wood shingles are popular in a variety of climates, and both can add architectural appeal to homes. If installed professionally, the homeowner can expect a reasonably long service life.

Both wood shingles and shakes, Photos 2-02 and 2-03 (above), are sawn on the bottom or

2-02 Wood shingle roof

2-03 Wood shake roof

2-04 Tile roof

2-01 Asphalt-composition shingles

2-05 Concrete tile roof

underside. However, a shake is split on the top face. In contrast, a wood shingle is sawn on the topside. This slight difference in manufacturing means that a shake has a much rougher, rustic look. In contrast, the wood shingle looks much more uniform. The difference in appearance is quite noticeable.

When roofing a home, climate often dictates that the "best material" be used over the "most appealing" material. In warmer climates, where the roof stays hot for long periods of time, concrete or clay tiles often are used. On the East Coast, slate roofs have been popular because of their stability in harsh winter conditions.

Both clay tiles and concrete roofs, Photos 2-04 and 2-05 (left), are durable, often lasting many decades. Both materials are likely to outlast asphalt shingles. However, installation is more complex and more costly. Also, both materials can be more expensive to repair.

Over the years, a number of composite shingle types have come and gone in the sloped roof market. Far less durable and more expensive to repair, many of them ended up on the losing side of class action lawsuits.

Flat or Low-Sloped Roofs

Coverings for flat or low-sloped roofs fall into a completely different category. Without slope, they cannot rely on a "fish scale" configuration to shed water. Dead-flat roofs often experience water ponding (accumulating) on parts of the roof.

One problem with standing water on the roof is that it is heavy. Water weighs 62.4 pounds per cubic foot, in fact. A 1-inch pond converts into 5 pounds per square foot. This adds an unnecessary load to the home's structure. The added weight could have serious results if not controlled. Another problem is that water can find its way through any small hole or crack in the roof and damage the home below.

No roof surface is purposely built completely flat anymore. Now, all roofs must have at least some slope. To fix this problem in older homes, tapered foam board insulation can be used to create a slight slope toward drainage points (roof drains or scuppers).

Existing dead-flat roofs require a watertight membrane running edge to edge in order to work effectively. For years, the popular covering was nicknamed "tar and gravel." The technical term for this type of covering is a "built-up roof." This is because the covering is built up from layers of roofing felt, each being sealed with hot tar. Several layers of tar and felt are laid down and covered with a final "flood coat" of hot tar. Small diameter pea-sized gravel then is embedded to protect the underlying layers of felt from sun and weather damage. When finished, the waterproof membrane should protect a home for years to come. Photo 2-06 (below) shows a typical gravel built-up roof covering.

As technology advances, so do low-slope roofing options. Today's neoprene, rubber, and other synthetics are proven materials for use as watertight membranes. Not only do they last longer, but they are also easier to install because they come in wider rolls. These wider sheets require fewer joints, making leaks less likely. Depending on the particular system, a single-ply membrane roof can be covered with gravel to protect it from the sun. Insulation also can be installed either under it (between it and the roof deck) or on top of it (between it and the gravel). Photo 2-07 (below) shows a single-ply membrane roof surface.

Another material used on flat roofs is urethane foam. Sprayed on the roof decking, the urethane quickly expands to form a layer of closed cell foam. The foam is great at insulating roof decks from heat. However, the foam itself does not fare well in the sun's rays and requires its own sprayed-on coat of protective material. The foam can help provide a needed slope to a flat roof, but it can be easily punctured. If your roof has urethane foam, we recommend regular and conscientious maintenance.

2-06 Built-up or tar and gravel roof

2-07 Single -ply membrane roof

Extending the Life of Your Roof

These tips will help you extend the life of your roof covering:

- Keep surrounding trees trimmed so they do not touch the roof. Branches that are heavy with snow or hit the house during high winds can damage a roof.

- Look for missing, out of place, cracked, or curled roof components. This is hard to do without going onto the roof, so we recommend leaving the roof walking to a professional, such as your Home Inspector or a roofing contractor. However, you can check the general condition of the roof by standing on a ladder placed at several locations around the edges of the roof. Another option is to use binoculars and inspect the roof from the ground.

- Make a habit of cleaning the roof's surface, gutters, and downspouts twice a year, Photo 2-08 (below). A good time is in late spring and again in autumn after the leaves have fallen. Also, make an immediate inspection after any violent storm.

Roof Flashings

The most common places for a roof to leak are where the roof covering (shingle, shake, tile, etc.) meets other surfaces or materials. Chimneys, plumbing vents, roof vents, and sidewalls should all be protected with seals called "flashings." Flashings, Photo 2-09 (below), should also be used on adjoining sidewalls and dormers, as well as where two adjacent roof slopes meet in a valley. These are all potential leak areas. Therefore, the proper installation of flashings is critically important.

After the flashings are installed, they should require little or no maintenance, and they should last the life of the roof covering. It is important to note that roofing cement is NOT a flashing material. If flashings or patches on your roof have been sealed with roofing cement, you should inspect these areas often and renew the seal frequently. When you check your roof, make sure to look for damaged or worn flashings. These should be replaced quickly.

2-08 Cleaning gutters and downspouts twice a year will help extend the life of your roof

2-09 Properly installed flashing should last the life of the roof covering

Section 2: Wall Cladding— Decorative and Functional

Exterior walls are one of the most decorative and protective parts of your home. Each material used on the exterior walls is called wall cladding. Wall cladding comes in various types, but each type is meant to repel moisture, protect the structure, and provide a strong, low-maintenance finish.

Masonry Walls

Many older homes (75 years or older) use the structure itself as the exterior finish. This is most common in homes with solid brick or stone masonry exterior walls. If you have an older home like this, try knocking on the inside face of your exterior walls. If the surface sounds solid and there is no hollow sound, you probably have a solid masonry wall with a plaster finish on the interior. Adobe and log style homes are two other examples of a structure that also serves as the exterior finish.

Wood and Wood-Composite Siding

Over time, more homes used wood to frame the structure. This method meant that a separate exterior wall cladding was necessary. Wood and aluminum siding, as well as brick and stone veneer all became popular choices.

Early wood siding was simply solid wood planking installed horizontally. Often, the bottom of each piece lapped over the outside face of the piece below. This was effective and referred to as "lap siding." Soon, other types of siding with overlapping grooves were developed. Their designs allowed water to wash down the exterior surface of the home and to be directed to the outside face of the cladding.

In the 1960s, siding made from wood byproducts began to replace wood siding. At first, these composites were made from glued sawdust and other lumber mill byproducts. Newer versions of wood composite siding use large wood chips glued together in a pattern similar to oriented strand board (OSB). Most wood byproduct claddings have a patterned face to make them look like a weathered wood plank.

In addition to plank siding, other wood cladding options include 4-foot-wide sheets of plywood or wood byproduct. Often made to look like grained wood, these sheets are installed vertically on the exterior. This cladding is popular on Tudor style homes. Some are even made to look like stucco.

If your home has wood or wood byproduct cladding, take careful note of the maintenance it will need. Remember that wood also may be used on trim, decks, and railings, as well as the exterior walls. Wherever natural wood is exposed to the sun, the sun's rays drive the natural oils out of the wood, causing it to dry out. This can result in checking (splitting along the grain), warping, and cupping.

However, if natural wood or any wood byproduct is shaded or sheltered from the sun, it may take on moisture. The moisture can lead to mold and rot the wood. Moisture is a serious problem, especially for wood byproducts. Long-term moisture problems can break down the sawdust, wood fiber, or chip-based composite to its original form, and your exterior finish will be destroyed.

To prevent these problems, composite wood siding must be constantly and completely sealed. A good coat of paint should be applied along all exposed surfaces. This includes the ends as well as the exposed bottom edges where the siding overlaps the piece below. By regularly checking the condition of the weather seal, and applying a protective finish when needed, you will ensure a long life for your home's wood siding.

One final note on wood composite siding: Recently, new materials have come onto the market that improve the durability of composite wood siding. One example is the use of portland cement to replace the various resins used to hold the wood composite siding together. Although siding using portland cement requires special equipment during installation, the result is a longer-lasting wall cladding.

Stucco

The use of stucco has long been popular in our western and southwestern regions. These homes can be easily identified by the use of chicken wire reinforcement under a multi-layer application. Photo 2-10 (below) shows a typical stucco exterior. This photo also highlights one of the advantages of a stucco finish: Stucco can be applied on curved surfaces and can be formed into soft, round corners.

2-10 Typical stucco exterior with weep screed

Notice how the face of the stucco wall extends out an inch or so beyond the underlying foundation. An important drainage function, this projection is called a "weep screed." This feature allows any moisture that might penetrate the exterior wall to "weep" out from under the stucco at the bottom.

Although stucco is a low-maintenance exterior wall cladding, any cracks should be sealed. This is especially important around windows, doors, and on horizontal surfaces. If you have a stucco home, you should frequently examine its exterior. Pay close attention to areas where moisture could penetrate. We recommend sealing cracks with a high-quality exterior grade caulking material. Urethane or silicone-based products work well.

Exterior Insulated Finish System

In the 1970s, an artificial stucco product called Exterior Insulated Finish System (EIFS) was introduced to homes. EIFS was marketed as a low-maintenance cladding that could be applied relatively inexpensively. Photo 2-11 (below) shows a home clad in EIFS.

EIFS is installed by first placing a 1-inch rigid foam insulation board onto the home's structure. The foam board is then covered with reinforcing fabric mesh. One or two layers of a cement-based slurry are then applied to form the exterior surface. In contrast to stucco's three layers that total anywhere from 1/2-inch to 3/4-inch, EIFS layers total from 1/4-inch to 3/8-inch. After the EIFS is installed, it will project over the foundation and look like a stucco "weep screed"; unfortunately, this projection does not provide the same drainage function as real stucco.

For this reason, over the past 10 years, EIFS has been the subject of many lawsuits and negative

2-11 Exterior Insulated Finish System clad home

press. On its own, EIFS works well as an exterior wall cladding. The problem is that after moisture gets behind the EIFS cladding and into the framework of the home, there is no provision for getting it back out. In numerous documented cases, moisture penetration and retention behind EIFS cladding has resulted in complete deterioration of structural wall sheathing. Even framing members such as 2 x 4 studs have been affected. This problem will remain until a solution for moving moisture out and away from EIFS-clad homes is devised.

If you own a home that has a cement-based exterior, we recommend that you find out whether your cladding is stucco or EIFS. Remember, stucco is applied over chicken wire mesh and is usually applied in three layers that total about 3/4-inch thick. Stucco also will have a weep screed around the bottom. If your cladding is thinner, applied over foam board insulation, and is reinforced with fabric mesh (often exposed along the bottom of the walls), then you may have EIFS. In that case, consider taking the following steps:

Have an expert confirm whether your home has EIFS. A qualified Home Inspector or an experienced EIFS specialist can help you. You want to make sure that the cladding on your home is, in fact, EIFS.

If you have any doubt about whether moisture has penetrated the walls (especially EIFS cladding), again, hire a qualified Home Inspector or qualified EIFS inspector.

Inspect the areas around penetrations in the cladding (windows, doors, vents, etc.) for small cracks. These cracks often form when the EIFS shrinks during the curing process. If any cracks are filled with caulking, check to see if the caulking has deteriorated.

Look for any softness in the wall by tapping on or gently pushing the cladding under windows.

If you believe any cracks are recent, or in a sheltered location—away from moisture—then seal the cracks with a high-quality caulking material and monitor them regularly.

As always, when in doubt, hire an expert! Structural damage caused by moisture trapped behind leaky EIFS is serious and can be costly to repair.

Remember, the main function of any exterior cladding is to keep moisture from penetrating the walls of your home. Forgetting to maintain the cladding can result in costly damage to your home. So, when in doubt, inspect, caulk, and paint! If any of these steps is outside your knowledge, hire a qualified expert.

Qualified Home Inspectors have nothing to sell but their expertise. They are paid to be your impartial advisor, and will have your best interests in mind.

Section 3: Garage Door Opener Safety and Maintenance

Your garage door opener is one of the most convenient appliances in your home. Although many openers provide years of faithful, trouble-free service, they still need to be maintained. If improperly adjusted, they can be expensive to replace—or even dangerous. Modern garage door openers are equipped with two adjustable features: length of travel and sensitivity to resistance.

The term "length of travel" means that the opener is adjustable for how far the door goes down to close and how far it goes up to open. Usually, the person who installed the opener made these adjustments properly. If the door or its installation changes for any reason, then the travel might need to be readjusted. Your owner's manual should show you how to properly adjust the travel.

The second adjustment is more critical. Your opener's "sensitivity to resistance" while closing causes the direction of the door to reverse and go back up. This feature is meant as a safety device. If the sensitivity is too strong, the door could continue downward and may harm a person or pet underneath. The sensitivity of the downward stop and reverse feature should be set so that a very minimum amount of upward pressure will be all that it takes to stop and reverse downward travel.

One suggested method for setting the downward stop and reverse sensitivity is to set a 2-inch by 4-inch piece of wood on its wide side on the floor in the path of the door. Then, the homeowner would check to see if the door stops and reverses when it touches the 2 x 4.

There are two problems with this test method. First, a wood board is strong and can provide almost unlimited resistance. The opener could still be adjusted to apply way too much force before stopping and reversing. This improper adjustment could easily break the bones of a child before the door reverses. Second, because the board is not flexible, it could permanently damage the door or cause it to jump off its track.

The method we recommend is that you catch the bottom panel of the door with both of your hands when the door is still a few feet from the floor. By applying upward pressure with your hands, judge how much upward force you are willing to tolerate before the door stops and reverses. The advantage of this method is that you can easily let the door go on downward if the pressure gets to be too great—before the door buckles or jumps off its track.

Unfortunately, many homeowners have the false impression that the light-beam sensor (in newer models) will reverse the travel once triggered by an object in its path. These sensors, mounted 4 to 6 inches off the floor of the garage, often get dirty and are not always a fail-safe method. You should test its operation periodically by deliberately interrupting the light beam to make sure that the door opener does, in fact, stop and reverse its direction of travel.

Photo 2-12 (below) shows a pair of sensors: one is a transmitter, the other is a receiver.

Transmitter   Receiver

Light beam completes the connection

2-12 Garage door sensors require an uninterrupted light beam from transmitter to receiver to work properly. Inset shows a transmitter and receiver on either pillar of a garage.

Section 4: Outside Hose Faucets

Outside hose faucets are called hose bibbs. Outside hose bibbs come in two basic types: "freeze-proof" hose bibbs, and conventional "non-freeze-proof" hose bibbs. In climates where it seldom or never freezes, freeze-resistant bibbs are not necessary; however, it is common to see both types.

Here is how to determine which faucet type you have. First, notice if the pipe connected to the handle runs straight into the body of the faucet. If it does, you probably have a freeze-proof hose bibb. In that case, the pipe runs from the faucet into the heated space of your home. If you see that the faucet has a shaft and handle projecting at about a 45-degree angle, it is probably a conventional or non-freeze-proof hose bibb, Photo 2-13 (below).

Photo 2-14 (below) shows a freeze-proof hose bibb. The cap on the top (behind the handle) is an anti-siphon device, which is now a required feature on all exterior hose bibbs.

If the winters are cold where you live, there are steps you should take to protect the outside faucets—even if you have freeze-proof hose bibbs. We will discuss these steps in the following paragraphs.

2-13 Non-freeze-proof hose bibb

Conventional Hose Bibbs

In cold winter climates, every conventional hose bibb should have a shutoff valve located safely inside the heated portion of the house. If you are having problems finding this valve, look for a drain port covered by a small screw cap. First, before winter sets in, you should shut off each of these inside valves. Next, remove the inside drain valve/cap on the side of the shutoff valve body. After you have done this, turn on the outside faucet so the pipe can fully drain. For the rest of the winter, leave the inside valve in the "off" position, and the outside conventional faucet "on." If the inside valve "weeps" over the winter, place a can or jar under the drain to catch any drips. In the spring, you need to reverse this procedure for turning the water back on.

A final note: Industry standards now require the addition of an anti-siphon device to any exterior hose bibb that was not manufactured with one. They are made to connect between your hose bibb and a hose. These devices can be obtained at any hardware or home improvement store.

"Freeze-proof" Hose Bibbs

Disconnect all hoses, water timers, splitters, and so on from your freeze-proof bibbs before the temperature drops below freezing. Leaving devices attached could trap water in the faucet's exterior cavity, where it can freeze and split the faucet housing. You may not discover a split faucet until the spring. Freeze-proof bibbs do not leak until they are turned on...so beware! Turning on a hose bibb with a split housing can flood the lowest levels of your home.

2-14 Freeze-proof hose bibb

Section 5: Winter Shut Down of Sprinkler Systems

In climates where it freezes each year, every outside sprinkler system should be shut down for the winter. To successfully shut down the system, proper draining is a must. If you are moving into your new home in the fall or winter and the home is located in a cold climate, you should confirm the status of winter shut down of the sprinkler system before closing on the house.

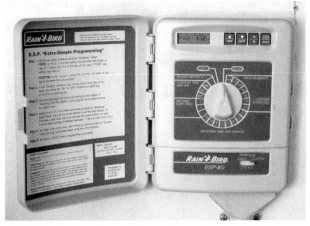

2-15 Typical sprinkler timer box

When and How to Shut Down a Sprinkler System

The ideal time to shut down the system is just before the first freezing weather. But, weather is difficult to predict—so is each system's reaction to colder temperatures. A skilled sprinkler system maintenance company in your area could probably best answer the question of "when." They also can best tell you "how."

In most cases, proper winter shutdown involves far more than just turning off a valve and opening a drain or two. Usually, a proper winter shutdown will involve opening all lines past the main supply shutoff and blowing out all circuits with compressed air. This becomes a ritual that you may not be equipped to handle; therefore, you should consider hiring an experienced sprinkler system maintenance company. The name of the company that installed the system is often printed on a sticker placed on the timer box, Photo 2-15 (left), or on a business card posted nearby.

Chapter 2 Conclusion

We covered a lot of material in this chapter, everything from roofs to garage door openers. Do not expect to learn everything about your home at once. Just pace yourself and keep this handbook as your guide. It takes a while to become a knowledgeable homeowner.

In the next chapter, we will explore plumbing.

IN CHAPTER 3

- How to add a bit of fresh air to your water

- Why washers can leak

- How to stop money from leaking down the toilet

- How to "dispose" of jams

Overview

You do not have to be a master plumber to perform some simple repair and maintenance tasks. In this chapter, we will explore some of the basics of plumbing: from simple tasks like unclogging and/or replacing an aerator to understanding why faucets leak. We will also explain how to replace washers or cartridges in your faucet. These step-by-step instructions, along with detailed photos and helpful tips, will not only save you money but also the bother of having a plumber come to your house.

Also included are tips on keeping your toilets in top shape along with a step-by-step guide on how to replace all their inner workings. We also cover suggestions on keeping your disposer from jamming and how to determine if it is an electrical problem or a plumbing problem if it does jam.

Information on water heaters will be included in this chapter. Questions like "Will I have enough hot water?" and "How much longer will my water heater last?" will be addressed. Also, tips on how to extend the life of a water heater with some simple yearly maintenance that just about anyone can do with ease. Water heater safety, and the importance of a temperature and relief valve, and what not to store around a water heater will be discussed

As with any procedure, only take on the tasks that you can safely and accurately accomplish. As always, if in doubt about anything regarding this chapter seek the help of a qualified or licensed professional.

Your Home Plumbing System Contains Several Components:

Kitchen

Bathroom

Laundry Room

Section 1: Aerator

The aerator is the little device that is screwed onto the spout of most bathroom and some kitchen faucets. An aerator serves two main purposes. First, it adds air into the water. Second, it screens particles out of the water. Some aerators even come with a "low-flow" washer inside to help conserve water. To do its job properly, an aerator must be clean. If you see water coming out of the faucet sideways or out the air inlet, your aerator is dirty.

If you are moving into a newly built home, clean the aerators immediately. This will help rid them of any construction debris. Photo 3-01 (below) shows the internal parts of a typical aerator.

To clean an aerator, simply unscrew it from the faucet and take it apart. It is important to remember the order in which you took it apart so you can put it together again. If the aerator is coated with mineral deposits from the water, soak it in vinegar. Home improvement centers also have products to dissolve mineral deposits. If the deposits will not come off, you can replace the aerator rather inexpensively.

Section 2: Washers

Replacing faucet washers is a job that you can do yourself. It does not take much time or a lot of tools. However, before touching the faucet, remember to turn off the water supply! This is easily done by locating and shutting off the valve that controls the water supply to that fixture. In most cases, this will be at an "angle stop" on the wall in the cabinet beneath the fixture.

If you have older faucets, look for two circular, compressible rubber washers, Photo 3-02 (below). These washers wear down each time the faucet is used, so they tend to leak as they near the end of their lifespan.

Shaped like a disk, the primary washer stops the flow of water when the faucet is turned off. This washer is located on the inside end of the faucet stem near where the water comes out. When this washer begins to leak, you will have to turn off the water, remove the faucet handle, unscrew the bonnet nut, and remove the stem. Then, install a new washer and reverse the sequence.

The other washer is shaped like a ring and surrounds the stem just under the handle. Its function is to seal the faucet stem so it does not leak from the bonnet under that handle. Many times it is possible to stop the "bonnet washer" from leaking by tightening the "bonnet nut" under the handle.

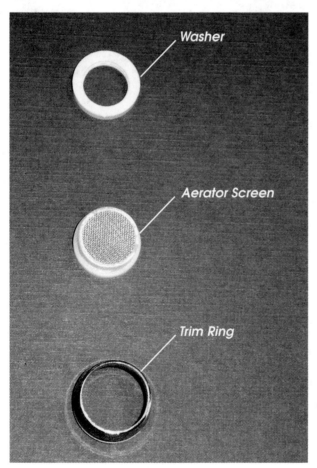

Washer

Aerator Screen

Trim Ring

3-01 Aerator components

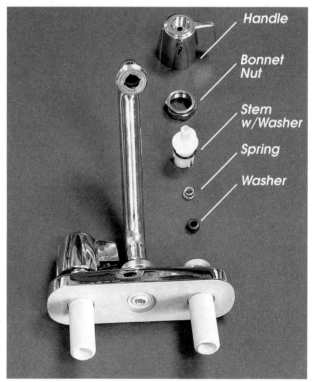

Handle

Bonnet Nut

Stem w/Washer

Spring

Washer

3-02 Washer

Section 3: Cartridges

Instead of washers, most modern faucets contain cartridges. These faucets are now known as "washerless faucets." Photo 3-03 (below) shows a typical cartridge for a washerless faucet.

Replacing a leaky faucet cartridge is an easy task. After you make certain the water has been turned off, remove the faucet handle, then the bonnet cap, and finally the cartridge itself. Take the old cartridge with you to the store to make sure you buy the right model.

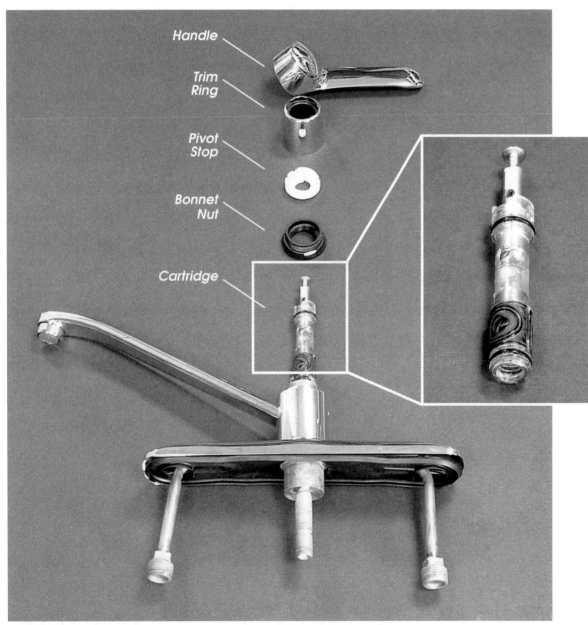

Handle

Trim Ring

Pivot Stop

Bonnet Nut

Cartridge

3-03 Faucet with replaceable cartridge

Section 4: Toilets

Keeping your toilet in good running order can help you save money on your water bill. A toilet is a fairly simple device with only two moving parts: (1) the flapper (or flush valve), and (2) the inlet valve. If either part is not working properly, the toilet could become unusable, or waste a lot of water. So, let's get a better understanding of each part.

The flush valve allows water to leave the toilet tank and flush the toilet bowl. Flush valves can be round rubber plungers (in older toilets) or rubber "flappers" (in more modern toilets), Photo 3-04 (below). The older rubber plungers attach to the bottom of a metal rod called a tank stopper. The new flappers drop over the hole in the bottom of the tank. Both valves are designed to stop the flow of water at the end of the flush cycle.

If your flush valve does not seal completely, the gap will allow water to trickle out of the toilet tank between flushes. This leak ultimately runs down the drain, wasting water. If the flush valve (plunger or flapper) is not closing completely, the inlet valve will periodically open to refill the tank between flushes. If this happens consistently, you will probably need a new flush valve.

The other moving part in the toilet is the inlet valve. This valve controls the water filling the toilet tank and maintains the proper water level for efficient flushing. If the inlet valve leaks continuously, the tank will fill to the top of the overflow tube, then overflow into the toilet bowl. From there, the excess water will flow out of the bowl and down the drain. Like a leaky flush valve, this can also be a big waste of water.

Replacing either of these valves is a task that can be done by a homeowner with a little time, patience, and the right tools. Again, the first step is to shut off the water. Locate the shut off valve (angle stop) that controls the supply to the toilet and turn off the water.

Second, flush the toilet to let the water out of the tank. If you are replacing the flush valve, follow the installation instructions printed on the package that came with the replacement.

If you are replacing the inlet valve, the next step will be to remove the rest of the water from the tank. Use a sponge or rag to stop the remaining water from flowing out of the bottom of the tank when the old inlet valve is removed.

Finally, follow the installation instructions that came with the replacement inlet valve. After you turn the water back on, pay careful attention to the water supply connection to the inlet valve. This is located under the tank. Also, look at the gasket that seals the inlet valve to the bottom of the tank. Make sure there are no leaks in these areas. The connection between the supply tube and the bottom of the inlet valve is particularly hard to seal because the water inside this connection is under constant pressure. If your installation passes the "leak test," then you have successfully completed this repair.

New pressurized tanks have no user adjustments, Photo 3-05 (below).

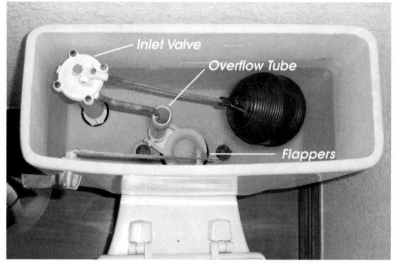

3-04 Typical toilet with "Flapper"

3-05 Pressurized toilet tank

Section 5: Disposers

If you are like most homeowners, you demand a lot from your garbage disposer. On occasion, we ask it to run without water, or overstuff it with food to grind up. Sometimes, objects that were never intended to be ground up (spoons, bones, and so on) find their way into the disposer. Through all of these conditions, most of us have come to depend on our disposers to provide years of faithful service.

What do you do if you flip the disposer switch one day and nothing happens? A couple of things could be going on, and you can fix it yourself by asking the right questions.

When you flipped the switch, did electricity flow to the motor? Did it hum? If the motor hummed, then it was receiving power, and the blades are probably jammed. If you still have your disposer's instruction manual, check to see what directions it gives for taking care of the jam.

If the manual is nowhere to be found, you can use a long, sturdy wooden stick, such as a broom handle, to reach the blades in the bottom of the disposer. Using a flashlight, try to locate any large, solid object that may be jammed between the sides of the disposer and the blades. Usually, you can get these objects loose by turning the blades (with the stick) in the opposite direction they turn when grinding up the garbage. **Never use your hands to turn the blades or remove objects.**

Another option is to look at the disposer from under the sink. Try to find a hexagonal recess in the center on the bottom of the disposer unit. This design allows you to use a "disposer wrench," Photo 3-06 (below), to un-jam the disposer blades. Use the wrench to turn the shaft in the direction opposite of the disposer's normal direction.

It is also possible that when you flipped the switch, there was no hum, which means no electricity was flowing to the disposer. If this happens, try to find the reset button on the bottom of the disposer. Pushing this button should reset the internal circuit breaker and restore the flow of electricity to the motor. If that does not work, check the disposer circuit breaker in your home's electrical panel. Normally, there is one circuit breaker in the panel just for the garbage disposer. Check it and make sure that that breaker is not tripped (turned off).

If un-jamming the blades and restoring power to the disposer motor does not fix the problem, you probably should contact a professional. If you can hear a hum, call a plumber. If no hum, call an electrician.

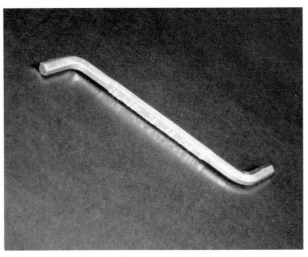

3-06 Disposer wrench

Section 6: Water Heaters

When it comes to water heaters, homeowners usually have two basic questions: (1) Will I have enough hot water for my family's needs, and (2) how much longer will my water heater last?

The first question, are we going to have enough hot water, is hard for anyone outside your immediate family to answer because so much depends on the number of people in your home, their ages and activities, and preferences for baths or showers.

There are, however, some rules of thumb about hot water heater capacity. For example, the majority of single-family homes in the United States built in the last 50 years were equipped with a single 40-gallon water heater. This fact alone indicates that any tank-type water heater with a capacity less than 40 gallons could be inadequate to support an average family's lifestyle.

In more recent years, many homes have been equipped with 50-gallon water heaters. Some newly constructed homes, particularly those with one or more jetted bathtubs, may feature two 40-gallon or two 50-gallon water heaters installed side by side and working in tandem, Photo 3-07 (below).

Other factors may also influence the water heater's ability to provide an adequate supply of hot water. These include the condition of the tank's interior and, in the case of gas-fired heaters, the combustion efficiency of the burner. When we mention the condition of the tank's interior, we are talking about mineral deposits. Specifically, as mineral deposits increase, heating efficiency decreases. Minerals can line the interior of the tank or, if the water heater is electric-powered, minerals can encrust the exterior heating elements.

To keep your water heater running efficiently, we recommend regular and frequent flushing of

3-07 Two 50-gallon water heaters

the heater. This step can be accomplished by rapidly opening and closing the drain valve. How often this should be done depends on the mineral content of your water. At a minimum, the bottom of each tank should be flushed once a year. If the water has a high mineral content, tanks may need to be flushed every other month. In summary, the buildup of minerals is the often the culprit behind the shortened life of a home water heater.

To return to the original question, having enough hot water for your family will depend on the size of the water heater and the maintenance performed on that heater. Only you can determine the right size of water heater for your family.

The second question of how long a water heater will last is somewhat easier to answer than the question of whether your family will have enough hot water. On a nationwide basis, water heaters tend to last an average of eight to 12 years. Still, several factors influence the service life of any given heater. In contrast, a few areas of the country have water with such a high mineral content that water heaters last only around three years.

Water heaters usually find their way to the landfill by springing a leak from the tank. Leaks typically occur where the tank has rusted through. However, if the water has a high mineral content, deposits on the bottom of the tank keep the heat of the flame from being transferred through the shell and into the tank. This condition results in overheating the tank bottom, causing the metal to fatigue and, ultimately, fail. The result is a large puddle on the floor surrounding the water heater. To summarize, a water heater can fail because the tank has rusted through or because the bottom gave way from metal fatigue. A water heater will not last forever, but by maintaining it and treating the water, if necessary, it can provide an ample supply of hot water and have a long life.

The previous paragraphs have focused on gas-fired water heaters. However, there are water heaters that are powered by electricity. Electrically heated water heaters have some unique characteristics of their own. Most electrically heated units larger than 10 gallons are equipped with two electric heating elements. Each element is located in the side of the tank: one near the bottom and one closer to the top. These heaters usually operate one at a time with the top element heating first and the bottom element finishing the job. Often, one of these electric elements will burn out leaving the whole job to the remaining element. Fortunately, when this happens, replacing the burned out element is all that is necessary to bring the water heater up to full operation once again. Sometimes, it is possible for one element to burn out without anyone in the home even noticing it; however, when the second element burns out everyone will know because there will be no hot water.

Some Important Information Regarding Water Heater Safety

For your family's safety, the water temperature control on every water heater should be adjusted to the lowest setting that provides sufficient hot water at showers and bathtubs. This is usually recommended to be **no greater than 120 degrees Fahrenheit**. Water temperatures above this can quickly cause second- and third-degree burns on adults. For example, **130°F water can burn in only 30 seconds; 150°F water can burn in only 1-2 seconds**. Children and the elderly can be burned even more quickly.

T&P Relief Valves and Discharge Tubes

Every water heater should be equipped with a "Temperature and Pressure Relief Valve," like the one shown in Photo 3-08 (below).

These safety devices have been a required part of every water heater installation since the 1940s. As a matter of fact, one is required by every manufacturer's warranty and by all local building departments.

As its name implies, a Temperature and Pressure Relief Valve can react to either (or both) excessive pressure or a too high water temperature. Almost a hundred years ago, when gas-fired water heaters were first sold for installation in homes, the primary concern was that excessive pressure could cause the tank to rupture. So, the first safety devices reacted only to relieve excessive pressure. Later, extensive testing by the manufacturers of relief valves confirmed that the real

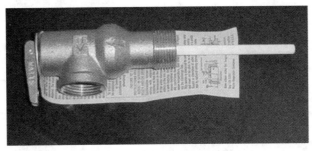

3-08 Temperature and pressure relief valve

destructive potential of excessive heating came from the energy stored up when water under pressure was heated too much; this discovery led to Temperature and Pressure Relief Valves. The white "shaft" projecting from the inside of the valve, in Photo 3-08, is the temperature-sensing probe. A proper installation will place the opening for the Temperature and Pressure Relief Valve in the top six inches of the tank, so all water heater manufacturers place the threaded opening either in the top of the tank, or in the side near the top.

All relief valves should be equipped with a discharge tube whose opening should be within 4 to 6 inches of the floor at the base of the heater, or the tube should discharge in a safe location where scalding water could not splash on a nearby person if the valve would suddenly open.

What Are You Storing Around Your Water Heater?

Water heaters are often placed in a closet or a mechanical room somewhere in the home. Too often, these locations also become attractive places for storing cleaning and other supplies. These might include flammable compounds, such as furniture polish, charcoal lighter fluid, mineral spirits, floor polish, disinfectant, glues, hair spray, and even gasoline or propane gas. In general, it is not a good idea to store anything—even nonflammable items—in the vicinity of your water heater.

Although a can of flammable liquid may not break or spill on the floor, it still could give off flammable vapors that often settle to the floor. You may not detect the smell of these vapors, but they are dangerously close to the pilot light for the water heater. These vapors could reach the pilot light before you realized the problem and the result would be disastrous.

Many water heater manufacturers have taken steps to avoid this serious problem. Most new water heaters comply with a voluntary standard that went into effect on July 1, 2003, which calls for them to be "Flammable Vapor Ignition Resistant" (FVIR). If your new or replacement water heater is designed to these standards, it is less likely to start a fire from nearby vapors. Still, we still strongly recommend against using the water heater location as a storage space.

Chapter 3 Conclusion

We hope the information in Chapter 3 will help maintain your plumbing and give you the confidence to tackle simple plumbing repairs.

IN CHAPTER 4

- Why you should know what is hanging over your head

- How to avoid common electrical mistakes

- Why smoke detectors and other alarms can be life-saving features

Overview

In this chapter, we will discuss some important electrical topics. One of the most important topics that will be covered is the distance to overhead electrical service wires. These are the wires coming into your home. Wires that are too close to the ground can be an obvious hazard to anyone who comes into contact with them. We will answer some of the most often asked questions about electrical safety. We will then discuss ground fault circuit interrupters (GFCIs), circuit breakers, and and portable GFCIs.

We talk about "Aluminum Wiring," when and where it can be safe and where it might be a safety hazard.

We describe the many different kinds of "Main disconnects" and why it is important to know where yours is and how to safely turn it off.

We also cover common electrical applications in the house, including switched electrical outlets, protected exterior outlets, floor mounted electrical outlets, 3-way switches, and the proper mounting of ceiling fans.

We conclude with a section on smoke alarms along with carbon monoxide alarms and propane gas alarms.

More so than in the other chapters, electrical issues can confuse and frighten a lot of people because electricity can be dangerous, can cause severe injury and even death. As with any procedure only take on the tasks that you can safely and accurately accomplish. As always, and especially in this chapter, if in doubt about <u>anything</u> regarding this chapter seek the help of a qualified or licensed professional.

Sections 2, 3, 4, and 5 reprinted with permission from the May/June 1992 issue of the IAEI News, published by the International Association of Electrical Inspectors, 901 Waterfall Way, Suite 602, Richardson, Texas 75080-7702.

Your Home Electrical Systems Involve Several Components:

Overhead Wires

Circuit Breaker

Applications in the Home

ELECTRICAL SYSTEMS AND SAFETY

CHAPTER 4

Section 1: Overhead Wires

Keeping wires out of reach is necessary for your safety and the safety of your loved ones. Wires that are too close to the ground or too near decks and porches, Photo 4-01 (below), pose serious hazards. The outcome of tangling with an electrical wire can be devastating.

The standard minimum "clearance" requirement for overhead wires in your yard is 10 feet. Clearance simply means that you must have a 10-foot distance from anywhere you stand before reaching the wires. Driveway clearance should be at least 12 feet. Over pools, the clearance is 18 feet (remember that long aluminum pole on the pool cleaner?). The horizontal clearance from a deck or porch to overhead wires is 3 feet. These clearances are vital because of the high voltages carried by the wires. In addition to making sure you have adequate clearance, it is also a good idea to look over the insulation covering the wires. The sun can dry out the insulation to the point where it may fall off, leaving the wires exposed.

The following four situations could develop into hazards. Look for these potential problems in your yard:

• Decks and balconies, Photo 4-01 (below), added to the home after initial construction. If a deck or balcony is added, the distance to the overhead wires may need to be adjusted.

• Wires passing through or around trees, Photo 4-02 (below). In time, these wires may sag toward the ground.

• Loose "anchorages." Anchorages hold electrical wires to poles or roofs. Because of age or storms, the anchorages could disconnect.

• Overhead wires running to a detached garage, shop, or barn that are not at least 10 feet above the yard, Photo 4-03 (below), along their entire length. Wires often sag as they age, and their anchorages can pull loose.

4-01 Wires too near balcony

4-02 Wires passing through trees

4-03 Sagging overhead wires

Section 2:
A Lifesaver—The Ground Fault Circuit Interrupter (GFCI)

If an inexpensive electrical device were properly installed in every United States household, nearly 70 percent of the approximately 240 electrocutions that occur each year would be prevented.

This life-saving device is called a ground-fault circuit-interrupter, or GFCI.

An unintentional electrical path between a source of current and a grounded surface is referred to as a "ground fault." Ground faults occur when current is leaking somewhere. If humans provide a path to the ground for this leakage, they can be seriously injured or electrocuted. Ground faults are often the result of damaged cords or appliances, poorly insulated wires, or mishandling, such as dropping an appliance in water.

GFCIs are products designed to prevent injury or death from electrical shock by detecting ground faults at very low levels. If a GFCI senses even minimal current leakage in an electrical device, it assumes a ground fault is taking place. It then interrupts the power fast enough to prevent injury to anyone in normal health.

To comply with the National Electrical Code, many homes built since 1973 have some GFCI protection. However, the U.S. Consumer Product Safety Commission (CPSC) estimates that as many as 70 percent of all existing dwellings have no such protection.

Several of the nation's leading electrical safety organizations, such as the CPSC, NEMA (National Electrical Manufacturers Association), and UL (Underwriters Laboratories, Inc.), encourage all consumers to equip their homes with GFCIs. Recommended areas to protect are kitchens, bathrooms, garages, crawl spaces, unfinished basements and outdoor receptacles—areas where many electrical hazards exist.

A consumer has three types of GFCIs to choose from for home use: wall receptacle, circuit breaker, and portable plug-in.

The three types of GFCIs designed for home use are readily available, inexpensive, and rather simple to install. Modern electronics and engineering practices, coupled with very rigorous functional testing standards, have made contemporary GFCIs durable, reliable, and extremely effective.

Wall Receptacle

Photo 4-04 (below) shows a front view and Photo 4-05 (below) shows a rear view of a typical wall receptacle type GFCI. It is used in place of a standard receptacle found throughout the house. It fits into a standard outlet box and, when properly wired, protects against ground faults whenever an electrical product is plugged into it, or any other receptacle supplied from it. Convenience outlet circuits in homes commonly consist of several (up to five or six) receptacles "daisy chained" together so that power is supplied from the circuit breaker protecting that specific circuit to the first receptacle in the chain. From there, power is carried on to the next receptacle, then on to the next, and so forth, until it reaches the last receptacle in the chain.

4-04 Ground fault circuit interrupter, wall receptacle, front view

4-05 Ground fault circuit interrupter, wall receptacle, back view

GFCI outlets are readily available at any home improvement center and many other stores, and it is physically possible for a homeowner to purchase and install one. However, we recommend that a competent, licensed electrician do any work on your home's electrical system that involves exposure to live components. However, if you do decide to tackle the installation of a GFCI receptacle, keep the following in mind:

GFCI receptacles are manufactured with two sets of terminals on the back. These sets are plainly marked, "Line" and "Load." The reason for two sets of terminals is to allow the GFCI receptacle to actually provide GFCI protection to any other receptacles supplied from it—remember the "daisy chain"?

In every case, however, no matter whether the receptacle you are working on is the first or the last receptacle in the daisy chain, the wires that bring the electricity to the receptacle must be connected to the terminals marked "Line"!

If the receptacle that you are replacing supplies other receptacles farther along in the chain, then the wires supplying the downstream receptacles must be connected to the terminals marked "Load."

We cannot overemphasize the need to properly wire GFCI outlets! These receptacles have complex circuitry that allows them to provide life-saving protection. If one outlet is wired incorrectly so that the electrical supply is not connected to the Line terminals, then it will not work properly. This usually means the receptacle itself is not GFCI protected and will not protect you when you need it most. Do not assume that if the "test" button works that the outlet is properly installed.

As stated earlier, electrical components in your home can be very dangerous. Many people prefer to play it safe and hire a licensed electrician.

Circuit Breaker

In homes equipped with circuit breakers, a GFCI circuit breaker, Photo 4-07 (below), may be installed in a panel box to give protection to selected circuits. This type of GFCI serves a dual purpose. It shuts off electricity in the event of a ground fault. It also will trip when a short circuit or an overload occurs. A qualified electrician should install GFCI circuit breakers in the home.

Portable

Portable GFCIs require no special knowledge or equipment to install. One type contains the GFCI circuitry in a self-contained enclosure with plug blades in the back and receptacle slots in the front. This type can then be plugged into a receptacle, and the electrical devices are plugged into the GFCI. Another type of portable GFCI is an extension cord combined with a GFCI, Photo 4-08 (below). It adds flexibility in using receptacles that are not protected by GFCIs.

After a GFCI is installed, it must be checked monthly to make certain it is operating properly. Units can be checked by pressing the "Test" button. The GFCI should disconnect the power to that outlet. Pressing the "Reset" button reconnects the power. If the GFCI does not disconnect the power, you should call an electrician.

Consumers whose homes are unprotected by GFCIs should consider having them installed either in receptacles or in their circuit breaker panel boxes. GFCIs also should be used whenever operating electrically powered garden equipment and electric tools.

4-06 Typical circuit breaker

4-07 GFCI circuit breaker

4-08 Portable GFCI

Section 3: Illuminating Facts About Home Electrical Systems

Answers to the Most Often Asked Electrical Safety Questions

What are some warnings of electrical hazards that I should be aware of?

Dim or flickering lights, arcs, sparks, sizzles and buzzing sounds, odors like the smell of burning plastic, switch and receptacle plates that are warm to the touch, cracked or loose plugs and wall plates, damaged insulation, frequent tripping of circuit breakers or blown fuses, and electrical shocks. If you notice any of these warning signs, you should call a licensed electrician.

How can I protect myself from electricity related injuries?

Look for problems in your home's electrical systems. Outlets and extension cords should be checked to make sure they are not overloaded. You should examine electrical cords to make sure they are not frayed or damaged or placed in spots where people may trip over them. You should make sure that the proper wattage light bulbs are being used in light fixtures and lamps. Consider installing GFCIs—ground fault circuit interrupters. One of the most important precautions you can take is to make sure the batteries in your smoke detectors are working properly. You can perform minor repairs, such as changing a fuse or circuit breaker, as long as you follow appropriate safety precautions and the manufacturer's instructions. To change a fuse, make sure that you replace the fuse with one of the proper ampere rating. To change a circuit breaker, check the panel for any sign of corrosion. For both, dry hands and a dry floor are necessary. Note: Where it is found that removal of the panel board cover may present some problem for you, we suggest that a licensed electrician be contacted to replace a defective circuit breaker.

Are there any benefits to using circuit breakers instead of fuses?

There are no safety advantages to having circuit breakers instead of fuses. The main difference is that circuit breakers can be reset, while blown fuses must be replaced. If a circuit breaker trips, simply reset it. If a fuse blows, first turn off the main power. Then, replace it with a fuse of the correct amp rating. Never put a penny or other metal object behind or in place of a fuse. Before resetting the circuit breaker or replacing the fuse, you should unplug all electrical products used on that circuit. Then, plug in each electrical product one by one after the circuit is operating properly. Before touching anything, make sure your hands and the floor are dry. If your breakers trip or your fuses blow repeatedly, call a licensed electrician because this may indicate a problem in your electrical system.

Why are there circuits with varying power ratings in a house?

Some larger household appliances, such as washers, dryers, stoves, refrigerators, and air conditioners, draw more current and have their own circuits. You should never plug in additional appliances with any of these products—doing so could overload the circuit.

What are the risks of overlamping (using a light bulb with a higher wattage than recommended by the manufacturer)?

Using a light bulb with a wattage rating higher than that recommended by the manufacturer could create a shock hazard or increase the risk of fire. Read the marking on the product or the use and care booklet to determine what wattage light bulb is suitable for the product.

How does a three-prong plug work? What is the benefit of using one?

The three-prong plug on a three-wire cord provides a path for electricity from an electrical product to leave the product.

How does a polarized plug work? What is the benefit of using one?

On a polarized plug, one of the "blades" on

the plug is larger than the other. A polarized plug properly aligns energized and neutral wires to reduce the risk of an electric shock. Some appliances have them, based on the type of product and its use.

What size extension cords should I use? How can you tell if an extension cord is appropriate for the intended use?

Before buying an extension cord, consider how the cord will be used. Will it be used with more than one appliance? Considering all the uses for an extension cord will help you answer the question of whether it is appropriate. But, you also should take care not to overheat the cord by overloading the rated electrical load. To determine whether there is a potential for cord overload, check the wattage rating on the cord. Then, add up the wattage ratings of all the products that will be operating at the same time on the cord. If the wattage rating on the cord is lower than the wattage rating of the products, eliminate one of the loads and check whether it is safe to use the remaining products with the extension cord. (If the wattage rating is not on the product, multiply the number of amps by 125 to determine equivalent watts.) UL-listed cords contain instructions for use as well as safety information. Extension cords smaller in size than No. 16 AWG should not be used around the house without appropriate over-current protection.

What does AWG mean on an extension cord? What does 13 A, 1625 W mean on an extension cord?

AWG means American Wire Gauge. It designates the size of the copper wire in an extension cord. The most common sizes for extension cords are 16 AWG, 14 AWG, and 12 AWG. The smaller the number, the heavier the wire. "13 A, 1625 W" means 13 amps, 1625 watts. Never plug more load (appliances, portable tools, and so on) than the specified number of watts into the cord.

What are GFCIs? What is the benefit of using them?

GFCIs, or ground-fault circuit interrupters, are explained in more detail in Section 2. The following gives you a brief overview of GFCIs. GFCIs function very simply: They constantly monitor electricity flowing in the circuit to detect a loss of current. If the electricity flowing through the circuit differs in the slightest amount from that flowing back, the GFCI will quickly shut off the supply of current flowing through that circuit. The advantage of using GFCIs is that they can detect even the smallest variations in the amount of electrical current—even amounts too small for your fuse or circuit breaker to detect, and then shut off the circuit. In addition, GFCIs work quickly, so they can protect consumers from severe or even fatal electrical shocks.

Can GFCIs prevent fires?

GFCIs may detect fire conditions caused by a ground fault or that result in a ground fault. The GFCI may shut off the power before the fire ignites, thus preventing the fire from spreading.

What are the present industry requirements for GFCIs?

In new construction, as well as in major renovations of older homes, present industry standards require GFCI protection in bathrooms, kitchens, basements, crawl spaces, garages, and outdoors. Present industry standards also require protection of specific equipment, including de-icing and snow melting devices, and electrically operated pool covers and pool lighting. However, because many homes were built before these industry requirements went into effect, the U.S. Consumer Product Safety Commission estimates that as many as 70 percent of existing dwellings may lack GFCI protection.

Do all GFCIs work the same way?

All GFCIs work in the same manner to protect you from ground faults. However, the circuit breaker type GFCI acts a bit differently from the receptacle and portable GFCI. The circuit breaker GFCI also provides overload protection for the electrical branch circuit. You can tell if your home has circuit breaker type GFCIs by looking at the electrical panel box. Unlike the regular circuit breakers, the GFCI circuit breaker has a TEST button.

If the GFCI is working, is there any danger of electric shock?

Even with the GFCI working properly, you can still be shocked. However, the GFCI acts quickly to limit your exposure to shock and protects against serious injury and electrocution resulting from ground faults.

What is the big plug now found on some appliances like hair dryers?

The large plug found on some appliances can be (1) an appliance leakage circuit interrupter (ALCI), (2) an immersion detection circuit interrupter (IDCI), or (3) a ground fault circuit interrupter (GFCI). They work in different ways, but they are all intended to shut off the power to an appliance under abnormal conditions, such as the appliance falling into water. Just because you have an appliance with one of these devices, it does not mean that it is okay to drop the appliance in water. The rule that "electricity and water do not mix" still applies.

If an appliance has a built-in shock protector, is an additional GFCI necessary?

Appliances that have built-in shock protectors may not need additional GFCI protection. However, other unprotected appliances would need GFCI protection.

If a product has a three-prong grounding type plug, is a GFCI necessary?

GFCIs are necessary even if the product has a third wire ground. GFCIs provide more sensitive protection to people against electric shock hazards. With grounding systems, if ground path degradation occurs, the high resistance could limit the current flow to ground below that required to trip the circuit breaker or blow the fuse. This would lead to a shock hazard if a person contacted energized exposed metal parts.

When purchasing a GFCI, what factors should I consider?

First, consider whether the GFCI carries the UL listing mark or that from some other recognized testing laboratory. For a circuit breaker GFCI, the make and model of the panel box determine whether the GFCI will fit the panel box. Recently, a combination

light switch/receptacle type GFCI has become available. This is for bathrooms where the only receptacle outlet is in the lighting fixture. A consumer can replace the light switch with a combination switch/receptacle GFCI.

How do you test a smoke detector?

Smoke detectors have a test button. Pressing the button does not necessarily mean that the detector works. Often, it simply shows that the battery in the detector works. To test a smoke detector, follow the manufacturer's instructions. The detector, Photo 4-09 (below), should be tested monthly, and the batteries should be replaced at least once a year or when the battery's low warning sounds, whichever comes first. Some permanently wired smoke detectors have battery backups, in case of power outages. These batteries must be checked once a year.

4-09 Smoke Detector

Section 4: Aluminum Wiring— Then and Now

For many homeowners and home buyers, the words "aluminum wiring" are cause for immediate alarm. This reaction is unwarranted and premature unless specific conditions that affect the safety of such wiring are present. It is far more productive to understand the nature and characteristics of aluminum wiring. It also may be helpful to understand why and when aluminum wiring was once accepted and widely used in home wiring, and why its use was eventually restricted. Aluminum wiring still meets present day industry standards and local codes in specific limited applications, because in those applications it is still considered safe and adequate.

Aluminum wiring was widely used in home electrical systems from around the mid-1960s until its use was significantly limited in the mid-1970s. During this period, aluminum wiring was cheaper and more readily available than copper. However, after a decade or so of "field trials" in the form of use (and abuse) by electricians and homeowners, aluminum was found to be a less than ideal replacement for copper in home wiring systems. Aluminum has several characteristics that make it less desirable than copper for many specific residential electrical wiring applications.

The Characteristics of Aluminum Wire

The following are among the less desirable characteristics of aluminum wire:

- A higher resistance to electrical current flow and lower ductility (which means the wire is less flexible),
- Incompatibility when placed in contact with certain other metals,
- Greater vulnerability to mechanical damage and damage as a result of oxidation,
- Greater sensitivity to temperature change (causing expansion and contraction), and
- Pressure sensitivity/flow.

All of these properties, if not clearly understood and respected when working with aluminum wiring, can lead to conditions that may damage the wiring and cause overheating at the area of damage. There are only two major potential safety hazards associated with any improper home electrical wiring conditions, regardless of the wiring materials used: excessive heat and electrocution.

Resistance

Aluminum's inherently high resistance (lower conductivity) to electrical current flow requires the use of larger-diameter conductors than would be necessary if copper were installed. For example: a number 14 gauge copper wire is adequate on a 110 Volt 15 Amp circuit, but a number 12 gauge aluminum wire is required for the same circuit (the smaller the gauge number, the larger the diameter of the wire).

Ductility

Aluminum is less ductile (or less flexible) than copper. This means that it fatigues and breaks more readily than copper when subjected to repeated bending. Therefore, much greater care is required when working with aluminum wire. As the wire fatigues, it breaks down internally which, in turn, dramatically increases its already higher resistance to electrical current flow. This results in an excessive heat buildup at the area of fatigue.

Compatibility

The incompatibility of certain metals when in contact with other metals causes a reaction known as galvanic corrosion. Simply put, one metal is eaten away by its contact with another. Galvanic corrosion occurs when aluminum comes in contact with certain other metals. This requires that care be taken to determine the component material of any outlet, switch, or other electrical device to which aluminum wiring is connected. If aluminum wiring contacts an incompatible metal, it will be damaged, resulting in increased resistance to electrical current flow and, again, heat buildup. To ensure that any outlet, switch, or other electrical device is compatible with aluminum wiring, the designation "CUAL" or "COALR" should be clearly visible on the device, or the device should be clearly specified by the manufacturer as being compatible with aluminum wiring.

Section 5:
Your Electrical Service Entrance— Always at Your Service

An important part of home safety is knowing when and how to turn off the power supply to the house. In general, this is done when work is performed on a home's interior wires.

Electrical power comes into your home either (1) overhead by way of a service drop, or (2) underground through a service lateral. It then passes through the meter and is usually conducted to a "main disconnect." The main disconnect may not be in a "main distribution panel" or "branch circuit panel." However, in many service areas, one can encounter many examples of a type of electrical distribution panel that was popular for residential use years ago called a "split-buss panel." Split-buss panels do not have a main disconnect that is capable of turning off all the power to the house with only one "switch." (In homes that have a main disconnect, the power can be turned off with one switch.)

In the paragraphs following, we will describe most of the commonly encountered types of service entrances. We hope that one description fits your home's electrical configuration.

Main Disconnect Located at the Meter

For single family dwellings, one common type of disconnect located at the meter is shown in Illustration 4-10 (below). In this configuration, the main disconnect is located in a separate enclosure that is usually placed immediately adjacent to the meter base. If the meter base is located on a pole, then the main disconnect enclosure usually is located immediately below it on the same pole. If the meter base is attached to the side of a house or garage, then the main disconnect enclosure is usually found immediately to one side.

Main Disconnect Located in a Multiple-Service Meter Bank

In buildings that contain more than one dwelling, such as duplexes, apartments, townhomes, and condominiums, the most commonly encountered service entrance is the "meter bank." A meter bank, as the name implies, is a cluster of meters located at one place, usually on the exterior of the building. Most often, the meter bank also contains the individual main disconnects for the various units within the building.

Each disconnect is normally located near the meter that measures the electrical power consumption for that unit. The challenge may be to find the specific meter for your unit. Often, the enclosures for the meter banks have been painted over many times and the enclosures may lack labels designating what unit is served by what meter and disconnect. Illustration 4-11 (below) shows a typical meter bank for a duplex home with the main disconnects located immediately below each meter.

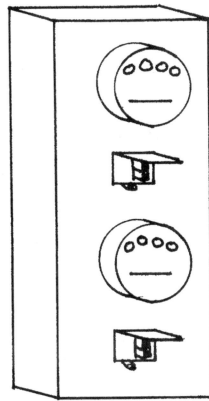

4-11 Main disconnect located at a multiple service meter bank

4-10 Main disconnect located in a "raintight" enclosure next to the meter

If the main disconnect is located near the meter (and, thus, is separate from the main distribution or branch circuit panel), then you usually will not find another main disconnect within the main distribution panel. The high-amperage double-pole circuit breakers usually employed as main disconnects often are considered to be too expensive to be used in duplicate applications. Instead, the main distribution panel will be without the familiar "main" in the top-center of the deadfront or panel board cover. Illustration 4-12 (below) shows a typical main distribution/branch circuit panel without an integral main disconnect.

Main Disconnect Located in the Main Distribution/Branch Circuit Panel

By far, the most common configuration has the main disconnect located in the main distribution/branch circuit panel. This configuration is shown in Illustration 4-13 (below).

Before proceeding, we should explain the different configurations of circuit breakers that are com-

monly found in home distribution panels.

The simplest and most-often used circuit breaker is the single-pole circuit breaker shown in the middle of the left side in Illustration 4-13-1 (below). These circuit breakers are used to protect 120-volt circuits. To save space, two single-pole circuit breakers often are combined or condensed in such a way as to only take up the space normally occupied by one full-sized single-pole circuit breaker. These are sometimes called "tandem" or "piggy-backed" circuit breakers. They are shown toward the bottom of the panel in Illustration 4-13-3 (below).

The two prevalent configurations are the stacked "half-width," shown in the left bank in Illustration 4-13-2 (below), and the "side-by-side," shown on the right bank in Illustration 4-13-3 (below). Many times, if a panel board is full of conventional single- and double-pole circuit breakers, a licensed electrician can substitute tandem circuit breakers for some of the larger single-pole circuit breakers and, thus, gain the capacity necessary to add circuits without having to replace the main distribution panel.

To draw 240 volts from a main distribution panel for supplying a major appliance, such as a

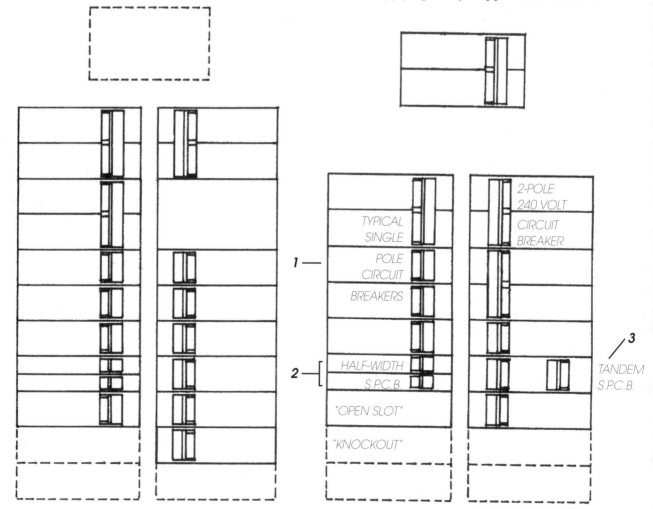

4-12 Branch circuit panel without a main disconnect (main disconnect located next to meter)

4-13 Branch Circuit Panel with Main Disconnect

kitchen range, clothes dryer, or electric water heater, a two-pole circuit breaker is necessary. These are shown in the top positions in the panel boards pictured on the preceding page. The usual convention is to place the two-pole circuit breakers at the top of the panel board with the 120-volt, single-pole circuit breakers arranged below.

Finally, the deadfront, which is provided to cover the face of the panel board, comes from the factory without any openings for the circuit breakers. Instead, the deadfront is partially punched or pressed leaving what are called "twistouts." As the electrician is installing and wiring the panel, an appropriate number of twistouts are removed by twisting them out with a pair of pliers so that the circuit breakers will be exposed through the deadfront.

If more twistouts are removed than necessary to expose all of the circuit breakers, or if later modifications of the circuit breaker layout are made, then open holes may be left in the deadfront. If open holes are left, it is possible for a careless person to put his or her fingers through the openings and contact energized electrical components. This action could easily result in serious injury or even electrocution. For this reason, open holes in a deadfront are considered to be a life-safety issue that demands immediate attention. These open holes can be safely covered with special plastic or metal covers that are made specifically to snap into these openings and protect fingers from the underlying live electrical components.

Split-Buss Panels

The last important type of electrical service entrance equipment that we will discuss is the split-buss panel. These panels were commonly used several years ago and may be found on either the interior or exterior of the house. Split-buss panels are distinguished by the fact that they do not contain a single main disconnect. Instead, they are divided into two separate sections: a main section, which is usually on top, and a lighting section, which is usually located below the main section. A split-buss panel derives its name from the fact that the buss bars, which are located in the back of the panel and which supply the electricity to the circuit breakers, are split (horizontally) somewhere near mid-height. The buss bars in the top half are energized all the time because there is no disconnect from their source of electricity.

Usually, the two-pole 240-volt circuit breakers that supply the dedicated circuits are located in the main section on this upper buss. The 120-volt branch circuits are fed from single-pole circuit breakers that are located in the lighting section on the lower buss. The lower buss does have a main disconnect, which is often labeled as the "lighting main" or "main for lighting." This main disconnect is located above the lighting section in the main section, Illustration 4-15 (left).

To turn off all of the electricity in the entire house, it will be necessary to turn off all of the circuit breakers in the main section. When the circuit breaker labeled "main for lighting" or "lighting main" is turned off along with all of the other circuit breakers in the upper (main) section of the panel, the electricity in the house should be totally shut off. A typical split-buss panel layout is shown in Illustration 4-14 (left).

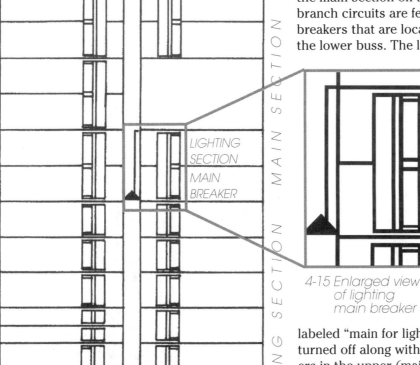

LIGHTING SECTION   MAIN SECTION

LIGHTING SECTION
MAIN BREAKER

4-15 Enlarged view of lighting main breaker

4-14 Split-buss branch circuit panel

Securing Outside Electrical Equipment

If your main disconnect or main distribution/branch circuit panel is located outside your home, it is possible that it can be accessed by anyone. A prankster could come along and pull the main switch for laughs. For you, such a sudden loss of power may be inconvenient—or even frightening. We recommend that you place an inexpensive padlock on the panel cover. In general, all you have to do is make your electrical panel less convenient for the prankster. In most cases, he or she will move on to find an unlocked disconnect.

Just remember that if you decide to sell your house in the future, you must have the key to the padlock ready to turn over to the homeowner and home inspector. Examining the main disconnect is an essential part of a competent and thorough home inspection.

The preceding information is reprinted with permission from the May/June 1992 issue of the IAEI News, published by the International Association of Electrical Inspectors, 901 Waterfall Way, Suite 602, Richardson, Texas 75080-7702.

Section 6: Electrical Applications Commonly Found in Homes

This section discusses important electrical applications that may already be used in your home. We will look at five categories in the following order:

• Switched electrical outlets

• Protected exterior outlets

• Horizontal outlets (mounted in floors)

• 3-way switched lights

• Proper mounting of ceiling fans

Standards require that there must be easy access to lighting when you enter a room. The only exceptions are closets. Usually, a wall switch near the room's door can turn the ceiling light on or off. However, in rooms where there is no ceiling light fixture, switched outlets (also called receptacles) are used.

The purpose of a switched outlet, Photo 4-16 (right), is to allow you to turn on a table or floor lamp by using the wall switch near the door. Just leave the lamp in the "on" position, plug it into a switched outlet, and the light will work. The duplex outlet is "split" so that one outlet is switched, and the other stays on all the time. If you are not sure if your rooms have any switched outlets, look for receptacles installed upside down. Sometimes, this is done so that the switched outlet stands out from the other outlets in the room.

Note: Dimmers are not permitted in switched outlet circuits; so, do not be tempted to replace a conventional wall switch with a dimmer if it is switching an outlet!

Outlet circuits in homes are commonly daisy-chained together (in groups of five or six). This means that power is supplied from the circuit breaker (protecting that specific circuit) to the first receptacle in the "chain." From there, power is carried on to the next receptacle, then to the next, and so forth, until it reaches the last receptacle in the chain.

Another type of switched outlet is called the GFCI, or ground-fault circuit interrupter. GFCIs can be life-saving devices and are covered in greater detail in Sections 2 and 3.

As stated earlier, electrical components in your home can be very dangerous. Many people prefer to play it safe and hire a licensed electrician.

4-16 Switched outlets provide additional safety and convenience

Protected Exterior Outlets

All exterior electrical outlets must be covered with an approved "weather-tight" cover, Photo 4-17 (below). The cover includes seals at the edges to prevent water from entering. If the receptacle is installed in a box mounted on an exterior surface, then the entire box and cover assembly must be weather-tight.

New industry standards require that these weather-tight covers be large enough to provide weather protection for any cords that may be plugged into the outlet. Instead of the weather cover only sealing the outlet opening when closed, as in the past, the cover must now protect the outlet and any cords plugged into it. Also, all exterior outlets must be ground fault protected.

Horizontal Outlets

Floor-mounted outlets provide power in the middle of a room. These outlets are commonly used in modern buildings, but also show up in additions to and retrofits of older homes. Floor outlets also can supply power to lamps or other devices that may be located far away from walls.

Floor outlets require a special box that is rated and approved for floors. Do not use wall outlet boxes or cover plates over floor-mounted outlets. They are not suitable to protect the outlet from heavy furniture, foot traffic, or moisture. Floor-rated covers are more expensive than wall covers, but they are necessary given the wear and tear they must endure.

Photo 4-18 (below) shows a typical floor-mounted receptacle. Notice the heavy brass cover with openings threaded for screw-in closures.

3-Way Switched Lights

As we discussed earlier, you must be able to turn room lights on or off by a switch near each room's entryway. But, have you ever turned on a light at the top of the stairs and then turned off the same light at the bottom of the stairs? Special circuitry, called 3-way switches, allows that to happen. In 3-way switched circuits, Photo 4-19 (below), the switches themselves are special devices, called "3-way," or "single-pole, double-throw" switches. This is because a third wire must run between these switches to enable the ceiling light to be operated from either switch.

Some homeowners incorrectly replace 3-way switches. They often install a single-throw switch or a dimmer switch instead of a 3-way switch. Single-throw switches use two wires instead of three. When a single-throw switch is installed, the 3-way circuit is disabled and the light can no longer be controlled from two locations.

By replacing 3-way switches on your own, you can mistakenly lose your lighting and no longer comply with industry standards. As with most electrical issues in your home, consider calling in a licensed electrician.

4-17 Protected exterior outlet

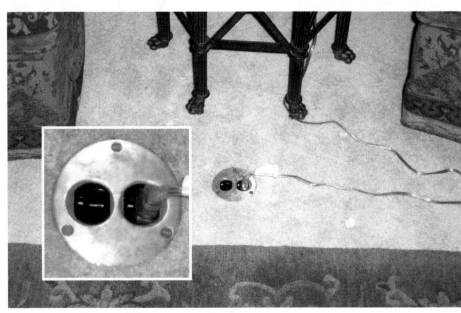

4-18 Typical floor-mounted receptacle

4-19 Three-way switch

Proper Mounting of Ceiling Fans

The last topic in this section is the mounting and support of ceiling fans. Ceiling fans, Photo 4-21 (below), have regained popularity in recent years. Many fans are being installed in older homes where they have never been used before. Even in homes with central air conditioning, ceiling fans can increase air circulation and make a room feel cooler.

Ceiling fans are heavy. In fact, they can weigh up to 50 pounds. Also, they can vibrate noticeably while running. For these reasons, ceiling fans should be installed in ceiling boxes, Photo 4-20 (below), that are rated to support their loads and movement.

These boxes are supported by the structural framing in the ceiling. Specially designed brackets are also required. Additional hardware inside the ceiling box attaches to the fan so that its weight is carried directly to the ceiling structure and not just into the box. If you plan to install a ceiling fan yourself, be sure to use a box that will hold the fan's weight. Do not depend on an enclosure that previously only supported a light fixture.

Home inspectors do not check to see if ceiling fans are supported by the appropriate boxes because these boxes are not readily accessible. To inspect the box, a person likely would have to remove the ceiling fan to see how it is supported. If you have any doubts about your ceiling fan or its support, contact a licensed electrician.

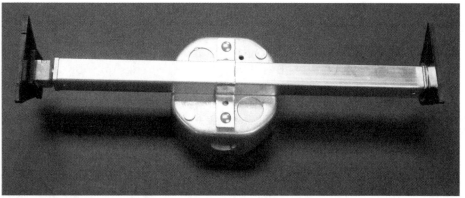

4-20 This ceiling fan box is specially designed to support weight and vibration.

4-21 Ceiling fans can weight up to fifty pounds and must be supported by the structural framing in the ceiling

Section 7: Alarms and Detectors

The final topic in Chapter 4 focuses on detectors and alarms. Included in this category are smoke alarms, carbon monoxide alarms, and propane gas alarms.

Smoke Alarms

Smoke alarms should be located inside every sleeping room as well as in the hallway immediately outside of sleeping rooms. They are also required in basements where stairways lead to a "dwelling unit," such as a den or bedroom.

Since 1979, smoke detectors installed in new homes must be "hard-wired." This means they are connected into the household electrical system. Since 1991, all hard-wired detectors also must have a battery backup. For older homes, battery-operated detectors are available. We recommend changing the batteries at least annually. You should check all of your alarms with their "test" buttons on a regular schedule. Smoke alarms, Photo 4-22 (below), should not be disabled just because they go off when the toast burns or cooking vapors from the kitchen trigger them. It is simply too easy to forget to turn them back on again. We recommend finding other methods to avoid false alarms, such as opening windows or doors to circulate air. In addition, never paint a smoke detector and keep it clear of cobwebs.

4-22 Smoke alarm

Carbon Monoxide Alarms

Tragically, thousands of people die of carbon monoxide poisoning each year. Carbon monoxide is a colorless and odorless gas, so you cannot rely on your senses to know it is around. It can also leak and build up in your home over time, causing major health problems. The number one source of carbon monoxide in homes is the practice of warming up an automobile in an attached garage. Clogged or disconnected flues are another source of carbon monoxide poisoning. The flue is the pipe that vents exhaust to the outside.

4-23 Carbon monoxide alarm

A major step you can take to safeguard your family is to install carbon monoxide alarms, Photo 4-23 (right), near fuel-burning appliances. Also, a home inspector can check your fuel-burning appliances and point out problem areas.

Propane Gas Alarms

Propane gas is heavier than air. Thus, when propane gas escapes from a leak in the fuel supply or a defective appliance, it settles to the floor. Because it is well below the "breathing zone" for people walking through the area, it often lies undetected for some time. At that point, it only takes a spark at this lower level to ignite a catastrophic explosion.

Propane alarms can greatly increase the safety of propane-heated homes. In general, these alarms include a valve that can shut off the supply of propane if a leak is detected. If propane heats your home, or is used for another purpose, we strongly urge you to install a propane gas alarm. The alarm should be installed on the lowest level where the propane is burned.

Chapter 4 Conclusion

Coping with electrical systems, gas appliances, or propane heat might make you nervous. That is a natural reaction. There are some risks that come with these systems. However, do not let fear stop you from making certain these systems are running correctly. Instead, take on only the tasks that you feel you can safely and accurately accomplish. For everything else, seek the help of qualified and licensed professionals. They can help you identify and solve problems and install vital safety devices or appliances.

IN CHAPTER 5

- How forced air systems can lead to quick warmth

- Why it can take a while to "warm up" to hot water heat

- How radiant heat warms but never burns

Overview

Most homes built in the last 100 years have one of three types of heating systems:

- Forced Air/Heat Pump. These systems heat the air, and then distribute the heated air throughout various rooms in the home.

- Hot Water or Steam. These systems heat water, then circulate the hot water or steam to radiators, baseboard convectors, or through coils in the floor of each room.

- Radiant Ceiling. These systems heat the home with thermal radiation. Electric radiant ceiling systems and gas fired radiant heaters warm the occupants (but not necessarily the air) in the space they serve.

In this chapter, we describe the main characteristics of each system, describing in detail how they work . We also cover the traits of fuel-fired heating appliances, describing how each different system works, along with detailed periodic maintenance instructions. We give you instructions on how to change your air filters, clean your coils, clean your humidifier, as well as how to bleed the air and keep the circulating pump properly lubricated on your hot water heating system.

As with any procedure, only take on the tasks that you can safely and accurately accomplish. As always, if in doubt about anything regarding this chapter seek the help of a qualified or licensed professional.

The Most Common Types of Heating Systems:

Forced Air

Hot Water or Steam

Radiant Heat

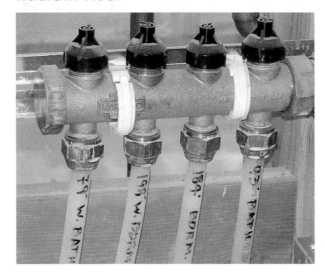

Section 1: Forced Air Systems

Usually heated with natural or propane gas, forced air systems are made up of several important components: the burners, a heat exchanger, and a blower. The burners' function is to burn the natural or propane gas inside the heat exchanger. The exchanger is a metal enclosure that separates the burners' flames from the air stream. The air stream is moved by the blower. The blower forces the heated air throughout the home's ducts to heat registers in each room.

A forced air system has several pros and cons. The greatest advantage is its quick response time. Forced air systems are capable of quickly heating your home to the setting on your thermostat. For many people, this system's tendency to dry out the air in the house is a big negative. In dry climates, some feel the need to add humidity to the air by installing supplementary humidifiers in the duct system or by operating portable room humidifiers.

5-01 Typical forced air furnace

Photo 5-01 (below) shows the interior of a typical modern forced air furnace. It is both easy and safe to remove the front access panel and blower compartment doors in order to do maintenance (as seen in the photo).

Another type of forced air heating system is the heat pump. A heat pump is simply a central air conditioning system with the added ability of "running in reverse." As a part of its design, the central air conditioning system can operate two ways:

- Remove the heat from your home and transfer it outside, or

- Operate "in reverse" to collect heat from the outside, condense it, and transfer it inside. Even if the outside air is 40 degrees, which is not exactly warm, this device has the ability to extract what little heat there is in the air, condense it into a coil, and redistribute into the house.

Heat pumps work best in mild climates, when the outside air temperature is above 40 degrees. Below 40 degrees, there is not enough heat in the outside air to bring into a home. However, most heat pump systems come with a backup called "auxiliary heat." The auxiliary heating device resembles a kitchen toaster. It has a bank of electric heaters inside its unit. This backup system works well when the outside temperature drops. However, the unit uses a lot of electricity and can quickly run up your electric bill. For this reason, heat pump systems are most popular in the warmer climates where there is seldom a need for auxiliary heat.

Keep these tips in mind if you own a heat pump system:

- Keep the filter clean year-round. Clean or replace the filter regularly (every 30 to 60 days or according to the instructions) during both the heating and cooling seasons.

- Next, do not run the system in the heating mode when the outside temperature is above 65 degrees Fahrenheit.

- Lastly, be kind to your wallet and do not run the auxiliary heat any more than necessary.

Air Filters

To run efficiently and safely, a heating system needs a clean air filter. In a gas burning forced air system, dirty or missing air filters can reduce efficiency. Dirt and dust slow the flow of air through the furnace heat exchanger and can cause it to overheat. This could shorten the life of the system or result in costly repairs.

The same care needs to be taken with a heat pump system. This system is made up of evaporator coils (hundreds of very thin, closely spaced, aluminum fins similar to an automobile radiator). When the air filter, Photo 5-02 (below), is dirty or missing, these coils act as a "substitute" air filter. Soon, the coils become clogged with dirt and an expensive service call is necessary.

When your system is in use, it is a good idea to check your air filter about every 30 to 60 days. Then, clean or replace the filter as necessary.

Installing Air Filters

Many of today's filters are disposable and come in a rectangular cardboard frame. If the filter has an arrow and the words "Air Flow" printed on the frame, then install the filter so that the arrow points in the direction that the air flows into the blower compartment. If your filter is installed at the base of the return air duct, which is on the side of the furnace, then the bottom of the return duct should have a sheet metal "angle" mounted near the outer side of the duct. (See Photo 5-02 below.) The base of the filter should be placed on the outside of this angle (the side farthest from the furnace). The angle helps hold the filter away from the blower compartment. The top of the filter then rests against the furnace side of the return air duct so that it leans at an angle across

the air stream.

This setup holds the filter in place and ensures it will filter all air coming into the furnace blower compartment.

Another type of air filter is called a "hammock" filter. With a hammock filter, the filter material must be at least 2 inches wider than the wire mesh basket it is installed upon. The wire mesh basket should be centered on the filter material. There should be extra material on both the front and rear to form a seal between the edge of the basket and the front door (and rear wall) of the blower compartment. Finally, keep in mind that the filter material goes on the outside of the basket.

Humidifiers

Forced air heating systems can dry out the air inside a home. To counteract dry air, some people use humidifiers. Furnace or duct-mounted humidifiers are able to restore some of the moisture that the heating system removes.

However, humidifiers, Photo 5-03 (below), do have some drawbacks. First, they must be cleaned regularly to remove mineral buildup and bacteria. Second, if the water supply to the unit is not properly controlled, humidifiers can leak water into the furnace. If the water lands on the heat exchanger, it will damage the furnace or cause it to need to be replaced.

So, if you already have or are thinking of installing a furnace-mounted humidifier, keep a watchful eye on the water supply. Also, clean the humidifier regularly.

5-02 Air filter

5-03 Humidifier

Section 2: Hot Water Systems

As the name implies, hot water systems use heated water to warm your home. The water is heated in either a gas-fueled boiler (natural or propane), or by electric elements submerged in a boiler. From here, the water is forced through one or more loops, or zones, by a circulating pump. The water then gives up its heat through coils in the floor, or fin-tube baseboards along the walls at floor level. In multiple-zone systems, the water flow in each zone is independently controlled by a zone valve. These valves then are controlled by a thermostat located in a room within that zone. Photo 5-04 (below) shows the boiler in a typical hot water heating system.

The main advantage to a water heating system is that the system can be split into multiple zones. There is a thermostat for each zone, which can be set at a different temperature. Also, hot water systems do not dry out the air in the home. Therefore, humidifiers are not likely to be needed.

The main disadvantage is that hot water systems take much longer to warm up a home than forced air systems. Depending on the size of the room, it may take half an hour or more to reach a comfortable temperature. Some people think they can speed up the process if they turn the thermostat up higher. This is not true: It just overworks the boiler and results in an uncomfortably hot room. We recommend that you find a comfortable temperature for each zone, set the thermostat, and leave it there.

Hot water heating systems have several moving parts that require attention. Newer systems tend to be complex. If you own a newer system, we recommend that you work with a qualified heating and cooling specialist to learn what maintenance you should do yourself. It is likely that the only task you will have to perform is to bleed any trapped air out of the circulation system.

In older systems, the circulating pump should be lubricated at least once a year. In addition, the expansion tank should be purged at least every other year. Section 3 outlines the steps for accomplishing these tasks.

5-04 Hot water heater gas fueled boiler

Section 3: Hot Water Heating Systems— Maintenance Steps

1. Securing the Thermostat

All thermostats in your home should be kept in a level position. They need to be secured to the wall so that the thermostat housing does not move when the temperature-adjusting pointer is moved.

A level thermostat is even more important if it uses a mercury switch. Mercury switch thermostats are easy to identify. Carefully remove the snap-on cover. You should be able to see the switching and control mechanisms inside. If the switch is a ball of mercury inside a sealed glass vial, then your thermostat is a mercury switch type. You should always mount and keep the thermostat in a level position.

2. Bleed the Air From the System Periodically

The next step is to bleed the air from the system. In most hot water heating systems, at least one air bleed device will be located in the distribution piping just above or near the boiler. The bleed device looks like an automotive tire valve (complete with cap), so it should be easy to find. Each of these air-bleeding devices should be opened once a year, or as necessary, to release any air trapped in the system.

Note! Be sure to close the air bleed as soon as the air has been released or water will begin to spray out!

3. Don't Let the Expansion Tank Get "Waterlogged"

Next, locate the expansion tank and its isolation valve (if so equipped). Then, decide whether you have a newer style or an older style expansion tank. Older tanks, which were typically installed before the '70s, usually are gray in color and are cylinders about 3 feet long and 12 to 16 inches in diameter. These cylinders are mounted high above the boiler. Newer tanks usually are blue or white in color, are much rounder in shape, and usually are not mounted as high up.

The following applies to older-style expansion tanks only. Your system may have an expansion tank with a valve between it and the distribution system. If it does, then you should close this isolation valve once a year, and drain all of the water out of the expansion tank. After draining the tank, close the drain valve and reopen the isolation valve to allow system water to again partially fill the vessel. Keep in mind that if the backflow preventer in the makeup water supply (or the relief valve on the boiler) "weeps" every time the boiler fires, you may have a "waterlogged" expansion tank. If this process of isolating, draining, and refilling the expansion tank does not stop the weeping, you need to call a plumber or heating technician to correct the malfunction.

Please note that while newer-type expansion tanks may not require much maintenance, when they do break, it usually means it's time to replace them.

4. Leave the Makeup Water Supply Turned "On"

Remember too, that the isolation valve and the makeup water supply valve should always be left on, except in an emergency. In general, if you have to close one of these valves because of a leak (or other problem), then you should call a plumber or heating technician immediately.

5. Keep the Circulating Pump Properly Lubricated

Some circulators on the distribution system are factory sealed and, therefore, cannot be oiled. If your system is not factory sealed, you should lubricate the oiling points once a year. A few drops of electric motor oil or non-detergent machine oil can be used. Just be careful not to over-oil, because you may end up with an oily spot on the floor.

Section 4: Traits of Fuel-Fired Heating Appliances

5-05 High and low combustion air pipes

All fuel-fired heating systems, such as forced air and hot water, have several traits in common. For starters, the fuel requires air for combustion. To sustain this combustion, the air must be in proper proportion to the fuel. In older homes, the air came into the home through gaps in the exterior walls and leaks around windows and doors.

Newer homes have "tightened up" and eliminated many of the leaks and gaps that allowed air into a home. Now, there is less air available for the furnace. To bring air into the home, air ducts run from the home's exterior and extend to the furnace and water heater.

The ducts are made of sheet metal. Usually, one duct is brought in near the top of the room that houses the heating system. Another duct discharges near the floor. These ducts also prevent the fuel-fired appliances from creating a mild vacuum, which might draw radon gas into the home. Combustion air is so important to modern fuel-burning appliances that many now pull their own dedicated supply of air from the exterior through a system of polyvinyl chloride (PVC) plastic piping.

No matter how air is brought into the home, it must flow smoothly to the appliances. Unobstructed airflow is vital for a furnace or water heater to run properly. Therefore, air ducts and grills must stay open year-round, even in severe winters.

Photo 5-05 (left) shows how the air that is needed for combustion is commonly brought into the home to discharge near the furnace.

In the Midwest and East, fuel oil has been the energy source of choice for furnaces, boilers, and even some water heaters. All oil burners share the following traits in common:

- A fuel pump to supply oil to the burner

- A blower to force combustion air through the burner to the vicinity of the nozzle. At the nozzle, it mixes with the atomized oil to form a flammable mist

- A method of ignition to start the whole process

The fuel-air mixture is critical for the burner to run efficiently. The burner has many moving parts, all of which must be properly adjusted. The entire oil combustion system should be cleaned, adjusted, and "tuned" on an annual basis. We highly recommend calling a professional experienced with oil-burning appliances for this task.

Section 5: Radiant Ceiling Heating Systems

The final type of heating system is radiant ceiling heat. This type of system is not common in typical homes. It is electrically heated and does not burn fuel. It warms objects in the room, not the air in the room. Radiant heat is flexible in that each room can be controlled with its own thermostat. However, like hot water systems, there is a long delay before the objects in the room warm up. Again, our advice is to find a comfortable temperature setting for each room, set the thermostat, and leave it alone.

NOTE: Radiant heat uses electric wires embedded in the ceiling. Therefore, you must be careful when drilling or nailing into the ceiling. If one of the wires is pierced, you could damage the heating system for that room, and maybe the whole house!

It may be difficult—or even impossible—to fix a broken electric wire in the ceiling. All such repairs will be costly. So, before drilling, call an inspector or licensed electrician. He or she can show you where you can safely drill!

5-06 Radiant ceiling (embedded inside of ceiling)

Chapter 5 Conclusion

When temperatures dip, there probably is no appliance quite as valuable as your home heating system. It can keep you comfortable even on the coldest nights. Show your appreciation by taking care of your heating system. Learn what maintenance steps you can reasonably perform and call a professional to do the rest.

IN CHAPTER 6

- Why many people choose their air to be refrigerated

- How the power of evaporation can cool your home

- How a fan can ventilate your entire home

OVERVIEW

Home cooling systems come in many shapes and sizes. However, most fall into one of four main categories: (1) central air conditioning(the most complex of the cooling systems), (2) evaporative coolers, (3) whole-house fans, and (4) ceiling fans(the simplest of the cooling systems). Central air conditioning (or "refrigerated") systems are popular in humid climates and distribute cool air through a system of ducts and registers. Evaporative coolers work better in areas with low humidity. Whole-house fans are effective in drawing in cool air from the outside. Ceiling fans circulate the air within a room, making it feel cooler.ir within a room, making it feel cooler.

Cooling systems can be permanently installed on the roof, adjacent to the home, or inside the house. They can also be seasonal fixtures that are used only during hot summer months. In this chapter, we will detail each system and provide you with simple tips on cleaning, operating, and maintaining each device. We will also discuss when to run your system in the cooler months.

As with any procedure, only take on the tasks that you can safely and accurately accomplish. As always, if in doubt about anything regarding this chapter seek the help of a qualified or licensed professional.

There are Several Types of Cooling Systems for Your Home:

Central Air

Evaporative Coolers

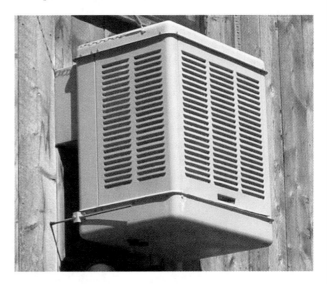

Whole House Fans

Section 1: Central Air/ Refrigerated Systems

Central air conditioning is the most complex cooling system of the four categories. Central air consists of a compressor/condenser unit as shown in Photo 6-01 (below), an expansion valve, and an evaporator coil. The noisiest part of the unit, the compressor/condenser is usually mounted on the ground next to an exterior wall. The expansion valve and evaporator coil are installed indoors. Some rooftop units have the compressor/condenser, expansion valve, and evaporator coil all built into the same unit.

The unit compresses refrigerant gas into a high-pressure, high-temperature gas. After it is condensed, the refrigerant flows into the home through copper tubing to the expansion valve at the evaporator coil. (The valve and coil are usually located in the plenum chamber of the furnace.) The expansion valve then expands the liquid back into a gas, which absorbs the heat from the passing air stream as it flows through the evaporator coil. Finally, a blower circulates the cool air throughout the home's duct system. (Usually, the same blower is used to distribute heated air during the winter.)

Both central air and window air conditioners cool the air using the same process. Window units have the same basic parts as a central air system. They simply operate on a smaller scale, and the cool air comes straight into a room, not through ducts.

Maintenance Tips

Taking care of your air conditioning unit starts with cleaning or replacing the air filter. Too much dirt can slow down the air flowing into the evaporator coil. In time, this can cause the coil to overcool, build up ice and freeze over. Dirt can also cause the closely spaced fins on the coil to act like a filter and clog, preventing adequate air flow and damaging the air conditioning unit. It also could damage the furnace if it shares the same ductwork with the air conditioner.

If your system's compressor/condenser unit sits on a pad next to your home, make sure that the pad (and compressor) stays level. Anything more than a 10-degree slant can permanently damage the compressor.

Other routine maintenance checks include the following:

- Maintaining insulation on the refrigerant lines.

- Keeping shrubs trimmed at least 2 feet from around the outside of the condenser unit.

- Not allowing lint from the clothes dryer vent, leaves or other yard debris to build up on the outside of the condenser fins. Debris may impede air flow through the unit.

6-01 Compressor/condenser

In addition, never run any type of air conditioner if the temperature outside is below 65 degrees Fahrenheit. Also, do not operate the air conditioner if the power to the compressor/condenser unit has been off for more than 24 hours (such as the unit being off waiting for a replacement part, or being off during the off-season) without first switching on the circuit breaker or re-installing the fuse(s) 24 hours in advance of turning the unit on. Operating the compressor under the wrong conditions can permanently damage the unit. It may even mean replacing the entire compressor, which is quite expensive.

On a more comforting note, if the air coming out of the air conditioning system is not 15 to 20 degrees cooler than the air going back in, do not panic. The most common cause for this problem is that the unit has lost some of its refrigerant. The solution usually includes recharging the system, which is a step that is far less costly than replacing the compressor.

Section 2: Evaporative Coolers

Evaporative coolers, Photo 6-02 (below), are popular in climates where humidity is low, because they are much less expensive to operate than refrigerated air conditioning. The following briefly describes how an evaporative cooler works and what its main components are:

- A pump draws water from a reservoir inside the cooler cabinet. A float valve maintains the water level in the reservoir.

- The water is then pumped through a tube until it reaches a "spider" attachment of hoses. The spider evenly trickles the water onto the vertical pads that line the inside of the cabinet. (The pads are made of materials that absorb water.) The water flows downward, saturating the pads, and collects again in the reservoir.

- The blower pulls outside air into the louvered sides of the cabinet, through the saturated pads (which cool the air), and distributes the cool air into the home through ducts or through a sleeve in the wall, ceiling, or window.

Maintenance Tips

To maintain your evaporative cooler, follow these steps:

- Keep the reservoir clean of dirt, debris, and mineral scale.

- Monitor the operation of the float valve and maintain all washers and seals. They are critical to shutting the water off completely when the reservoir is full.

- Make certain the pump is providing an adequate supply of water to wet the pads. Also, make certain the pump and the float valve are not encrusted with minerals from the water. If they become encrusted, it is usually cheaper to

6-02 Evaporative cooler

replace the parts rather than attempting to clean or repair them.

- Inspect the cooler for mineral buildup. If your water has a high mineral content, the spider inside the cooler often will become clogged and will prevent water from reaching the tops of the pads. We recommend that you periodically check all of the pads inside the cabinet to make sure that the pads are getting saturated.

- Check the circulation of cool air in all areas of your home. If the blower is not operating prop-erly, cool air will not be well-circulated. If the motor for the blower has oiling points, follow the manufacturer's suggestions for keeping them lubricated.

- Properly dispose of any overflow water. Each evaporative cooler should be equipped with an overflow pipe leading from the top of the reser-voir. The discharge from this overflow should be piped to a proper point of disposal. Overflow should not be allowed to simply spill onto the roof (if the unit is on the rooftop) or onto a patio or walkway.

Section 3: Whole-House Fans

A whole-house fan is a large fan that can venti-late your entire house. Whole-house fans, Photo 6-03 (below), are probably the simplest of all cool-ing systems to maintain. However, because the home's air is pulled into the attic, you must make sure that there is adequate ventilation to vent it from the attic. Whole-house fans push a large quantity of air out of the home. To avoid pressure building up in the attic, there must be sufficient roof and soffit vents to allow an equal amount of air to leave the attic. The problem of a buildup of pressure is mainly a problem in retrofit installa-tions where a whole-house fan has been placed in service after the home was initially built. Escape vents are essential and should be a part of your planning when installing such a fan.

Maintenance Tips

Other maintenance considerations for whole-house fans include the following:

- If the fan motor is equipped with oiling points, then they should be lubricated with a material and on a schedule specified in the owner's manual.

- If the fan uses a drive belt, the condition of the belt should be checked at least annually, usually at the beginning of the cooling season.

6-03 Whole house fan shown with louvers open and closed

• The moveable louvers should be lubricated with a material and on a schedule specified in the owner's manual.

We offer one final note of caution if you are planning to install a whole-house fan as a retrofit:

Do not cut any structural members in the process of installing the fan! All whole-house fans are manufactured in a way that allows them to be installed without cutting any structural member. Follow the manufacturer's installation instructions for every step of your installation.

Section 4: Ceiling Fans

As noted earlier, ceiling fans circulate the air within a room, which makes the room feel cooler. Ceiling fans, Photo 6-04 (below), require very little attention, and the maintenance tips below can help you get years of service from your ceiling fans.

Maintenance Tips

It is a good idea to occasionally vacuum any lint that has accumulated from around the ventilation air holes on the motor. If the fan develops a noticeable wobble, then balance it by following the instructions in the owner's manual.

Caution is needed if you are planning to install a ceiling fan in a site that only held a conventional light fixture. Ceiling fans are heavy. They should be mounted in and supported from ceiling electrical boxes that have been specifically made to support their weight. The boxes used to install conventional ceiling light fixtures are not designed to support a ceiling fan. Mounting a ceiling fan to a conventional electrical octagon box will probably cause its weight to pull the fan out of the box or the box out of the ceiling. In either case, the fan will fall and may cause great damage.

All retrofit installations of ceiling fans should include a careful examination of the box to which the fan is to be attached. If the box is not already rated for ceiling fan installation, it should be replaced with an appropriate box.

6-04 Ceiling fan

Chapter 6 Conclusion

The type of cooling system you have may depend on the climate where you live or simply on personal preference. Whatever system you currently have—or choose to install— can give you years of reliable service with simple maintenance.

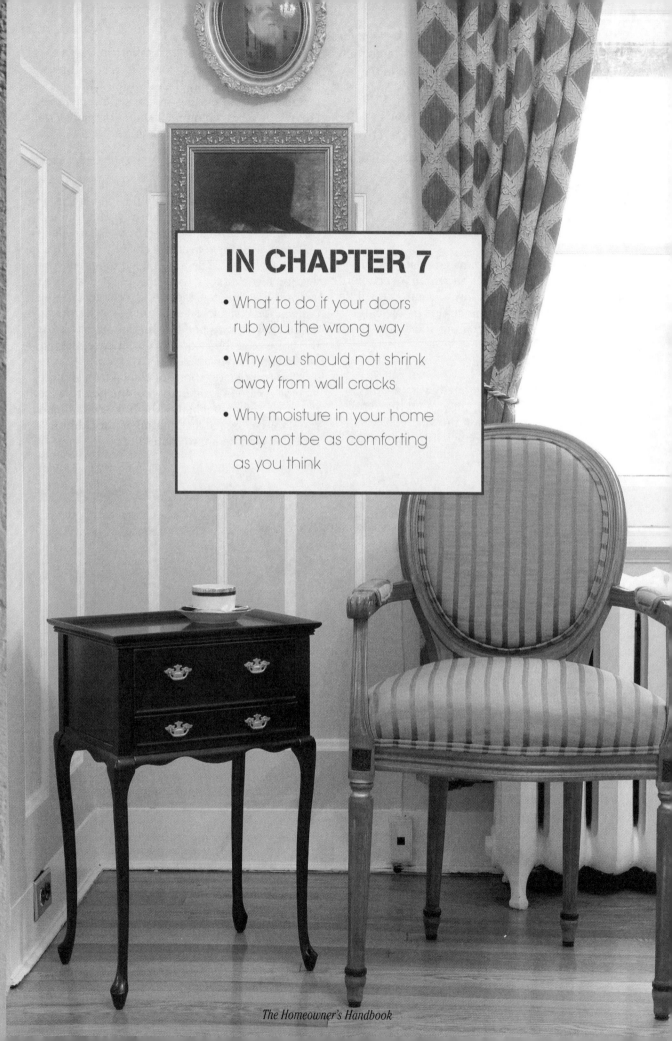

IN CHAPTER 7

- What to do if your doors rub you the wrong way

- Why you should not shrink away from wall cracks

- Why moisture in your home may not be as comforting as you think

OVERVIEW

In the previous chapters, the focus was on some of the basic, mostly exterior, components of your home: the foundation, exterior walls, the heating and cooling systems. In this chapter, the focus turns inward: to the interior of your home.

As your home ages some common, but not always major, problems can arise. Small, unsightly nail pops and shrinkage cracks can occur. We will detail how to determine the superficial ones from a structural problem, and how you can easily fix the superficial ones.

Other common problems that can happen are doors that rub on their frames and squeaky floors. Again, we show you how to differentiate between a nuisance and a structural problem. We will then make suggestions on how to correct the nuisance-type problems.

Other areas that are covered are the clothes washer water supply hoses, and why it is important to monitor them, along with the discharge standpipe and the importance of a clean dryer vent.

Other areas of consideration are indoor moisture management and ventilation including potential problems in your crawl space, basement or attic, where these problems may not been seen until some damage has already occurred. Also included is a seasonal home maintenance checklist.

As with any procedure, only take on the tasks that you can safely and accurately accomplish. As always, if in doubt about anything regarding this chapter seek the help of a qualified or licensed professional.

Interior Maintenance Keeps Your Home More Comfortable and Appealing:

Walls

Doors

Floors and More

Section 1: Dealing with "Signs of Maturity" in Your Home

As houses age, a variety of imperfections may come to the surface. Luckily, most of these signs of maturity can be easily fixed.

Nail Pops

Nail pops occur when the nails that are used to fasten the wallboard (or drywall) to the walls or ceilings are pushed out of the wooden framing. Usually, the nails only project about 1/16-inch from the wallboard. The good news is that while nail pops look unsightly, they are not a major problem.

Nail pops, Photo 7-01 (below), are often a sign that the wood used to frame the home is becoming older and dryer. When your home was built, the wood used to frame the home was "green," meaning it was new and contained a lot of moisture. As the wood ages, it begins to shrink and nails or even screws can be forced out.

Fortunately, you can easily and inexpensively fix nail pops. Simply use a small punch or nail set and hammer to drive the nail back into its original position. Then, cover the nail depression with a thin coating of resilient caulking material to restore the original surface finish or texture. If your home is relatively new, you may want to wait at least a year before fixing the nail pop. This will give the wood time to season, or shrink. By waiting, you may have to fix the nail pop only once.

Shrinkage Cracks

Shrinkage cracks in your ceilings or walls, like those in Photo 7-02 (below), can happen as a result of drying wood in the framing or drying joint compound. It is important, however, to know the difference between shrinkage cracks and cracks caused by structural movement.

In general, a shrinkage crack will be either vertical or horizontal in direction. In other words, the cracks follow the joints in the wallboard. Shrinkage cracks commonly show up in the drywall above windows or doors. With shrinkage cracks, the wallboard edges on either side of the crack are parallel, and the crack is seldom more than a hairline.

If your home has a crack in a wall or ceiling that is wider than a hairline, and especially if its two sides are not parallel, you may have a more serious problem. For example, your home's foundation may have shifted. We recommend consulting with your home inspector or structural engineer to determine the depth of the problem.

Patching shrinkage cracks is a simple process that you can easily accomplish. Simply fill the crack with a resilient caulking material and repaint as necessary. As with nail pops, it is best to wait until the home is at least one year old and has gone through all four seasons before patching these cracks. Notice that we have specified using a resilient caulking material for both shrinkage cracks and nail pops. This material is more durable and is less prone to shrinkage than drywall joint compound or spackle.

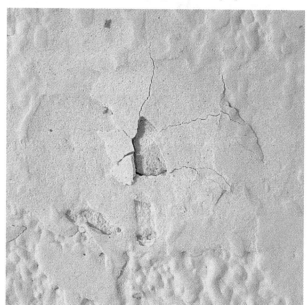

7-01 Nail pops are easy to repair

7-02 Cracks may be superficial or indicate a more serious structural problem

Doors That Rub on Their Frames

Doors that rub or drag on their frames are a nuisance. They can be difficult or even impossible to close. If your house was built by a professional, all of the doors should have been installed with a uniform distance between the door and its frame. Also, the frame should have been a perfect rectangle—not a parallelogram.

If a door and its frame were correctly installed and now the door does not close properly, then some outside force has distorted the frame. That force could be structural movement. Before fixing the door, we recommend that you first determine the cause of the problem.

If there has been structural movement, often there will be a diagonal crack in the wallboard radiating out of one or both of the upper corners of the door opening. Again, this is the time to work with a home inspector or other qualified professional. After structural movement has been ruled out or stopped, you can address the door problem. In minor cases, you can use sandpaper over the areas that rub. In more serious cases, the door may need to be planed or the door frame may need to be reset.

Squeaky Floors

Squeaking floors are caused by the subfloor moving over the top of the supporting joists when someone walks or moves heavy objects across the floor. Squeaking floors are less likely in newer high-quality homes since both nails and construction adhesive are now used to secure the subfloor.

The most permanent and practical cure for squeaking floors must wait until it is time to change the carpet or other floor covering. (This method does not apply to subfloors covered with hardwoods.) Before recovering the floor with carpet or tile, drive drywall screws through the old floor surface and into the joists below. (Make certain the screws penetrate into the joists.) After the connection is re-established between the subfloor and the joists, the squeaks will disappear.

Section 2: Considerations for the Laundry Area

Clothes Washer Water Supply Hoses

Just like the hoses in your car, the hoses that supply water to the clothes washer have a limited lifespan. In fact, the service life of some hoses is quite short. Many experts recommend replacing these hoses about every 2 years. Unfortunately, many homeowners replace the hoses only when a messy problem occurs. Do not make this mistake. Check your hoses for signs of wear and replace them periodically.

As with most products and services, you get what you pay for in washing machine hoses, Photo 7-03 (below). We recommend paying a little more and buying hoses that are reinforced with an external metal braid. Another good idea is to turn off the water supply to your clothes washer completely any time that you anticipate being gone from your home for more than a day.

Lastly, you may want to consider placing your clothes washer inside a metal pan equipped with a hose that leads to a floor drain. This is an especially good idea if the clothes washer is on a floor above the lowest floor in your home. The devices that control the water level in the washer tub have been known to stick open occasionally and overfill the machine. Also, some machines have been known to eject water from the tub during the spin cycle. Having an extra level of protection against a flooded room is a wise choice.

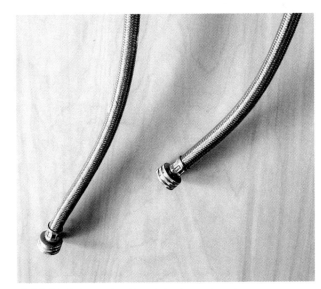

7-03 Stainless steel braided washer hoses

Discharge Standpipe Size

The standpipe is the drain pipe that takes the water discharged from the washer, Photo 7-04 (below). Homes that are more than about 25 years old often have standpipes with an inside diameter of 1-1/2 inches. Modern standpipes have an inside diameter of 2-inches. The problem with older standpipes is that modern washing machines discharge water faster than the pipe can accommodate. The combination of an older standpipe and a modern washing machine can mean wash water overflowing the standpipe and flooding the room. The only practical cure for this situation is to have a plumber install a larger diameter standpipe. Do not attempt to seal the washing machine drain hose into a smaller standpipe. This is impractical and unsanitary—and can be dangerous.

Dryer Venting to the Exterior

During the "energy crunch" of the 1970s, a number of devices claimed to save energy by making use of the clothes dryer exhaust and humidity. Most of these gadgets ended up simply dumping the exhaust into the home. However, the exhaust from any clothes dryer contains water vapor and lint. A buildup of lint is a fire hazard, and water vapor that collects on walls or ceilings can promote the growth of mold. If the dryer is heated with gas, the exhaust also contains dangerous byproducts, such as carbon dioxide.

Obviously, it is not a good idea to breathe dryer exhaust. Instead, make sure your dryer is properly vented, Photo 7-05 (right), to the exterior of your home. A "proper duct" has been defined as no more than 6 feet of flexible duct connected directly to the dryer itself. (If the dryer is heated by gas, the flexible duct must be made from metal.) The duct from the dryer must discharge into a 4-inch smooth wall sheet metal duct. The sheet metal duct must be routed by the shortest distance, with a minimum of elbows, to a hood on the outside of the house. Because lint can still build up in this system, you should frequently clean the dryer exhaust system.

7-05 Dryer vent

7-06 Shower vent fan with light

7-04 Discharge standpipe

Section 3: Indoor Moisture Management and Ventilation

Some humidity inside a home can be a comfort and a benefit. However, too much moisture can create problems for both people and property. Excess moisture can result from a number of problems, such as a pipe or washing machine hose bursting, a sewer system backing up, or a roof leaking. If excess moisture remains in any part of a home, furnishings and building components will begin to deteriorate. In some cases, mold and rot can occur and cause permanent damage.

For these reasons, you should conscientiously maintain the weather shell of your home. This means making sure the roof is not leaking and that moisture is not coming in through the exterior walls. Also, if water spills inside the home from a burst pipe or other problem, the water should be quickly removed and all wet areas should be thoroughly dried. Depending upon the extent of the spill, you may want to check the interior of stud cavities and other normally inaccessible areas. Moisture that gets into areas with little air circulation may rot framing members and grow harmful mold.

An often-overlooked source of indoor moisture is the everyday activities of washing dishes and clothes, bathing, and cooking. How often have you seen steam coming out of the vent at the top of your dishwasher door during the drying cycle? Many bathrooms, especially in older homes, have only a window for ventilation—and that window may be rarely opened. Many range vent hoods in kitchens merely recirculate the air they take in right back into the kitchen. All that moisture may make the kitchen seem warm and hospitable, but where it lands can cause damage in the long run.

In short, the moisture level (humidity) in the home must be kept at a rather low level. The most effective method for accomplishing this requires having—and using—kitchen, laundry, and bathroom ventilation systems, Photo 7-06 (left). These systems effectively carry moisture to the exterior of your home.

The attic is another area where good ventilation is vital. If the attic is poorly ventilated, then damage is almost certain to occur to critical roofing elements. Problems are especially likely to occur if the laundry or kitchen ventilation systems discharge into the attic. In extreme cases, the water vapor that makes its way into the attic can condense on the cold underside of the roof sheathing and then "rain" down on the ceiling insulation, damaging the wallboard in the ceiling itself.

To make certain that mechanical ventilation systems are functioning properly, try to check these items at least annually:

- Make sure that all exhaust ducting is properly attached to the vent fan housing and is sealed at every joint or connection, and that it goes to the exterior of the home.
- Make sure that the fan blades (or blower cage) and motor are clean and in good working order. (Many fan/motor assemblies can be unplugged in the vent housing and removed for cleaning.)
- Make sure that any filters, such as those in kitchen range hoods, are kept clean to allow for maximum air flow.

Finally, encourage all members of the family to use the ventilation fans whenever they are doing an activity that involves water.

Chapter 7 Conclusion

It may seem that there are many steps you must take to keep your home in running order. This is true; however, you need not feel overwhelmed. Instead, you may want to cluster certain maintenance tasks by season and set aside a few hours each quarter to accomplish these tasks. Having a regular maintenance routine can help spot and solve problems early. The maintenance checklist on the following page can help organize tasks.

You should also consider setting aside a portion of the household budget to pay for inevitable home repairs or routine inspections. Having the money on hand can help keep you from cutting corners on home maintenance.

Your home is likely to be your single largest investment and, like all investments, it needs to be carefully managed. By identifying and solving problems early, your home can grow in value and —more importantly—provide a safe, comfortable haven for you and your family.

Task	Spring	Summer	Fall	Winter
Inspect foundation, basement, or crawl space for cracks and note their direction. (See Chapter 1)	✔			
Clean gutters and downspouts. Also make sure water is draining away from the home's foundation. (See Chapter 2)	✔		✔	
Check roof for damaged shingles, shakes, or tiles and trim tree branches away from roof. (See Chapter 2)	✔		✔	
Prepare outside hose bibbs and sprinkler systems for cold weather. (See Chapter 2)			✔	
Inspect exterior walls for cracking and wear. (See Chapter 2)	✔			
Check for leaks in plumbing and make sure aerators are not clogged. (See Chapter 3)		✔		
Replace any worn faucet washers or cartridges. (See Chapter 3)		✔		
Inspect all electrical cords, wall plates, and plugs for damage and wear. (See Chapter 4)	✔	✔	✔	✔
Make certain electrical wires coming into your home have the required clearance and do not sag. (See Chapter 4)	✔			
Check all alarm systems (smoke, carbon monoxide, and/or propane gas) and make sure they are functioning properly. Replace batteries as necessary. (See Chapter 4)		✔		
Make certain all GFCI (ground fault circuit interrupter) plugs are functioning properly. (See Chapter 4)		✔		
Service heating and cooling systems. (See Chapters 5 and 6)	✔		✔	
Replace filters in heating and cooling systems. (See Chapters 5 and 6)	✔	✔	✔	✔
Inspect clothes washer hoses for wear or damage. Replace as needed. (See Chapter 7)				✔
Make certain any kitchen, laundry, and bathroom ventilation systems are functioning properly and any filters are replaced routinely. (See Chapter 7)				✔
Make certain the attic is properly ventilated and shows no signs of dampness. (See Chapter 7)		✔		
Clean the dryer vent duct. (See Chapter 7)		✔		✔

ENERGY SAVERS

Tips on Saving Energy & Money at Home

*Reprinted with permission as a public service.

Introduction

Did you know that the typical U.S. family spends close to $1,300 a year on their home's utility bills? Unfortunately, a large portion of that energy is wasted. The amount of energy wasted just through poorly insulated windows and doors is about as much energy as we get from the Alaskan pipeline each year. And electricity generated by fossil fuels for a single home puts more carbon dioxide into the air than two average cars. By using a few inexpensive energy-efficient measures, you can reduce your energy bills by 10% to 50% and, at the same time, help reduce air pollution.

The key to achieving these savings is a whole-house energy efficiency plan. To take a whole-house approach, view your home as an energy system with interdependent parts. For example, your heating system is not just a furnace— it's a heat-delivery system that starts at the furnace and delivers heat throughout your home using a network of ducts. You may have a top-of-the-line, energy-efficient furnace, but if the ducts leak and are uninsulated, and your walls, attic, windows, and doors are uninsulated, your energy bills will remain high. Taking a whole-house approach to saving energy ensures that dollars you invest in energy efficiency are wisely spent.

Energy-efficient improvements not only make your home more comfortable, they can yield long-term financial rewards. Reduced operating costs more than make up for the higher price of energy-efficient appliances and improvements over their lifetime. Improvements may also qualify you for an energy efficiency mortgage, which allows lenders to use a higher-than-normal debt-to-income ratio to calculate loan potential. In addition, your home will likely have a higher resale value.

This information shows you how easy it is to reduce your home energy use. It is a guide to easy, practical solutions for saving energy throughout your home, from the insulating system that surrounds it to the appliances and lights inside. Please, take a few moments to read the valuable tips in this booklet that will save you energy and money and, in many cases, help the environment by reducing pollution and conserving our natural resources.

Check levels of insulation in walls, ceilings, attic, crawl space, basement, and on the water heater.

Check for holes and cracks around windows, doors, light fixtures, outlets and walls

Check for storm windows or double-pane windows

When shopping for a new appliance, always check for the ENERGY STAR® label.

Whole-House Energy Plan

Prioritize your whole-house plan by viewing your home as an energy system with interdependent parts.

Your Home's Energy Use

The first step to taking a whole-house energy efficiency approach is to find out which parts of your house use the most energy. A home energy audit will show you where these are and suggest the most effective measures for reducing your energy costs. You can conduct a simple home energy audit yourself, you can contact your local utility, or you can call an independent energy auditor for a more comprehensive examination.

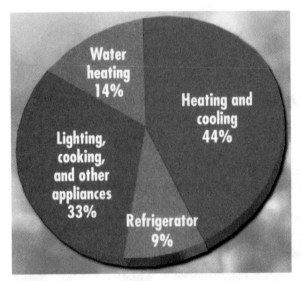

How We Use Energy In Our Homes (based on national averages)

The largest portion of a utility bill for a typical house is for heating and cooling.

Energy Auditing Tips

• Check the level of insulation in your exterior and basement walls, ceilings, attic, floors, and crawl spaces. Contact your local contractor for advice on how to check your insulation levels.

• Check for holes or cracks around your walls, ceilings, windows, doors, light and plumbing fixtures, switches, and electrical outlets that can leak air into or out of your home.

• Check for open fireplace dampers.

• Make sure your appliances and heating and cooling systems are properly maintained.

• Study your family's lighting needs and use patterns, paying special attention to high-use areas such as the living room, kitchen, and exterior lighting. Look for ways to use daylighting, reduce the time the lights are on, and replace incandescent bulbs and fixtures with compact or standard fluorescent lamps.

Formulating Your Plan

After you have identified places where your home is losing energy, assign priorities to your energy needs by asking yourself a few important questions:

• How much money do you spend on energy?

• Where are your greatest energy losses?

• How long will it take for an investment in energy efficiency to pay for itself in energy savings?

• Can you do the job yourself, or will you need to hire a contractor?

• What is your budget and how much time do you have to spend on maintenance and repair?

After you assign priorities to your energy needs, you can form a whole-house efficiency plan. Your plan will provide you with a strategy for making smart purchases and home improvements that maximize energy efficiency and save the most money.

Another option is to get the advice of a professional. Many utility companies conduct energy audits for free or for a nominal charge. For a fee, a professional contractor will analyze how your home's energy systems work together as a system and compare the analysis against your utility bills. He or she will use a variety of equipment such as blower doors, infrared cameras, and surface thermometers to find inefficiencies that cannot be detected by a visual inspection. Finally, he or she will give you a list of recommendations for cost-effective energy improvements and enhanced comfort and safety. A good contractor will also calculate the return on your investment in high efficiency equipment vs. standard equipment. For more information about home energy audits, contact:

U.S. Department of Energy's (DOE's) Energy Efficiency and Renewable Energy Clearinghouse (EREC)
(800) DOE-3732; (800-363-3732), www.eren.doe.gov/erec/factsheets

Finding a Contractor

When searching for a contractor, you should:

• Ask neighbors and friends if they have worked with a contractor they would recommend
• Look in the Yellow Pages
• Focus on local companies
• Look for licensed, insured contractors
• Get three bids with details in writing
• Ask about previous experience
• Check references
• Inquire with the Better Business Bureau

Cool ▬▬▬▬▬▬▬▬▬▬▬▬▬▬▬▬▬▬ Hot

Heat Loss from a House

A picture is worth... in this case, lost heating dollars. This thermal photograph shows heat leaking from a house during those expensive winter heating months. The white, yellow, and red colors show where the heat escapes, with the red representing the area of the greatest heat loss.

Thermogram/photograph copyright 1997, Infraspection Institute, Inc., Shelburne, VT

Your Home's Energy Use

Insulation and Weatherization

Checking your home's insulating system is one of the fastest and most cost-efficient ways to use a whole-house approach to reduce energy waste and maximize your energy dollars. A good insulating system includes a combination of products and construction techniques that provide a home with thermal performance, protect it against air infiltration, and control moisture. You can increase the comfort of your home while reducing your heating and cooling needs by up to 30% by investing just a few hundred dollars in proper insulation and weatherization products.

Should I insulate my home?

The answer is probably "yes" if you:

- Have an older home and haven't added insulation: in a recent survey, only 20% of homes built before 1980 were well insulated
- Are uncomfortably cold in the winter or hot in the summer—adding insulation creates a more uniform temperature and increases comfort
- Build a new house or addition, or install new siding or roofing
- Pay excessive energy bills
- Are bothered by noise from the outdoors—insulation helps to muffle sound
- Are concerned about the effect of energy use on the environment.

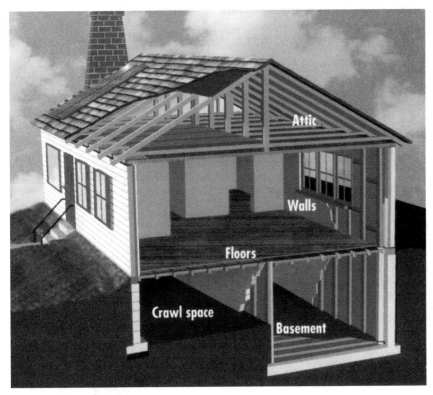

Where to Insulate
Adding insulation in the areas shown here may be the best way to improve your home's energy efficiency.

Insulation

First, check the insulation in your attic, ceilings, exterior and basement walls, floors, and crawl spaces to see if it meets the levels recommended for your area. Insulation is measured in R-values—the higher the R-value, the better your walls and roofs will resist the transfer of heat. The U.S. Department of Energy (DOE) recommends ranges of R-values based on local heating and cooling costs and climate conditions in different areas of the nation. For a more accurate and simpler method of determining your insulation needs, try the Interactive ZIP Code Insulation Program, which uses your zip code and some information about your house to tell you where to add insulation. The program was developed by the Energy Division of the Oak Ridge National Laboratory. State and local codes in some parts of the country may require lower R-values than the DOE recommendations, which are based on cost-effectiveness.

Although insulation can be made from a variety of materials, it usually comes in four types—batts, rolls, loose-fill, and rigid foam boards. Each type is made to fit in a different part of your house. Batts are made to fit between the studs in your walls or between the joists of your ceilings or floors. Batts are usually made of fiberglass or rock wool. Fiberglass is manufactured from sand and recycled glass, and rock wool is made from basaltic rock and recycled material from steel mill wastes. Rolls or blankets also are usually made of fiberglass and can be laid over the floor in the attic. Loose-fill insulation, usually made of fiberglass, rock wool or cellulose, is blown into the attic or walls. Cellulose is usually made from recycled newsprint treated with fire-retardant chemicals.

Rigid foam boards are made of polyisocyanurate, extruded polystyrene (XPS or blueboard), expanded polystyrene (EPS or beadboard), or other materials. These boards are lightweight, provide structural support,

U.S. Department of Energy Recommended* Total R-Values for New Construction Houses in Six Insulation Zones

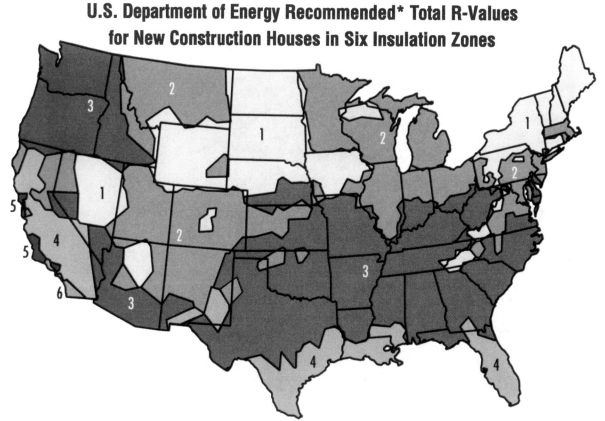

*These recommendations are cost-effective levels of insulation based on the best available information on local fuel and materials costs and weather conditions. Consequently, the levels may differ from current local building codes. In addition, the apparent fragmentation of the recommendations is an artifact of these data and should not be considered absolute minimum requirements.

The Homeowner's Handbook

and generally have an R-value of 4 to 7 per inch. Rigid board insulation is made to be used in confined spaces such as exterior walls, basements, foundation and stem walls, concrete slabs, and cathedral ceilings.

Insulation Tips

• Consider factors such as your climate, building design, and budget when selecting insulation R-value for your home.

• Use higher density insulation, such as rigid foam boards, in cathedral ceilings and on exterior walls.

• Ventilation plays a large role in providing moisture control and reducing summer cooling bills. Attic vents can be installed along the entire ceiling cavity to help ensure proper airflow from the soffit to the attic, helping to make a home more comfortable and energy efficient.

• Recessed light fixtures can be a major source of heat loss, but you need to be careful how close you place insulation next to a fixture unless it is marked. "I.C."—designed for direct insulation contact. Check your local building codes for recommendations.

• As specified on the product packaging, follow the product instructions on installation and wear the proper protective gear when installing insulation.

The easiest and most cost-effective way to insulate your home is to add insulation in the attic. To find out if you have enough attic insulation, measure the thickness of insulation. If there is less than R-22 (7 inches of fiber glass or rock wool or 6 inches of cellulose) you could probably benefit by adding more. Most U.S. homes should have between R-22 and R-49 insulation in the attic.

Zone	Gas	Heat pump	Fuel oil	Electric furnace	Ceiling Attic	Ceiling Cathederal	Wall (A)	Floor	Crawl space (B)	Slab edge	Basement Interior	Basement Exterior
1	✔	✔	✔		R-49	R-38	R-18	R-25	R-19	R-8	R-11	R-10
1				✔	R-49	R-60	R-28	R-25	R-19	R-8	R-19	R-15
2	✔	✔	✔		R-49	R-38	R-18	R-25	R-19	R-8	R-11	R-10
2				✔	R-49	R-38	R-22	R-25	R-19	R-8	R-19	R-15
3	✔	✔	✔	✔	R-49	R-38	R-18	R-25	R-19	R-8	R-11	R-10
4	✔	✔	✔		R-38	R-38	R-13	R-13	R-19	R-4	R-11	R-4
4				✔	R-49	R-38	R-18	R-25	R-19	R-8	R-11	R-10
5	✔				R-38	R-30	R-13	R-11	R-13	R-4	R-11	R-4
5		✔	✔		R-38	R-38	R-13	R-13	R-19	R-4	R-11	R-4
5				✔	R-49	R-38	R-18	R-25	R-19	R-8	R-11	R-10
6	✔				R-22	R-22	R-11	R-11	R-11	(C)	R-11	R-4
6		✔	✔		R-38	R-30	R-13	R-11	R-13	R-4	R-11	R-4
6				✔	R-49	R-38	R-18	R-25	R-19	R-8	R-11	R-10

(**A**) R-18, R-22, and R-28 exterior wall systems can be achieved by either cavity insulation or cavity insulation with insulating sheathing.
For 2 in x 4 in walls, use either 3-1/2-in thick R-15 or 3-1/2-in thick R-13 fiber glass insulation with insulating sheathing.
For 2 in x 6 in walls, use either 5-1/2-in thick R-21 or 6-1/4-in thick R-19 fiber glass insulation.

(**B**) Insulate crawl space walls only if the crawl space is dry all year, the floor above is not insulated, and all ventilation to the crawl space is blocked.
A vapor retarder (e.g., 4- or 6-mil polyethylene film) should be installed on the ground to reduce moisture migration into the crawl space.

(**C**) No slab edge insulation is recommended.

NOTE: For more information, see: Department of Energy Insulation Fact Sheet (D.O.E./CE-0180). Energy Efficiency and Renewable Energy Clearinghouse, P.O. Box 3048, Merrifield, VA 22116; phone: (800) 363-3732; www.ornl.gov/roofs+walls/insulation/ins_11.html or contact Owens Corning, (800) GET-PINK (800-438-7465), www.owenscorning.com

Insulation and Weatherization

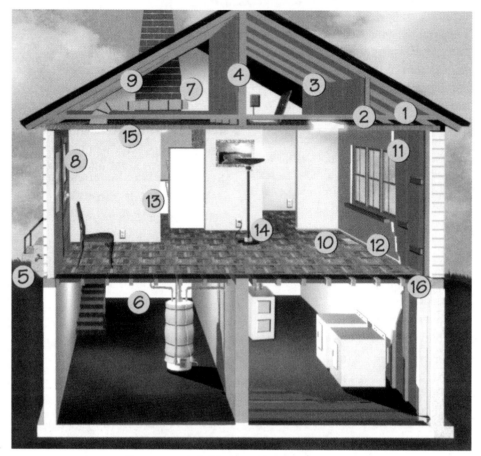

Sources of Air Leaks in Your Home

Areas that leak air into and out of your home cost you lots of money.
Check the culprit areas listed here:

1 Dropped ceiling
2 Recessed light
3 Attic entrance
4 Electric wires and box
5 Plumbing utilities and penetration
6 Water and furnace flues
7 All ducts

8 Door sashes and frames
9 Chimney penetration
10 Warm air register
11 Window sashes and frames
12 Baseboards, coves, and interior trim
13 Plumbing access panel
14 Electrical outlets and switches

15 Light fixtures
16 Sill plates

If your attic has ample insulation and your home still feels drafty and cold in the winter or too warm in the summer, chances are you need to add insulation to the exterior walls as well. This is a more expensive measure that usually requires a contractor, but it may be worth the cost if you live in a very hot or cold climate.

You may also need to add insulation to your crawl space. Either the walls or the floor above the crawl space should be insulated.

New Construction

For new construction or home additions, R-11 to R-28 insulation for exterior walls is recommended for most of the country. To meet this recommendation, most homes and additions constructed with 2" x 4" walls require a combination of wall cavity insulation, such as batts and insulating sheathing, or rigid foam boards. If you live in an area with an insulation recommendation that is greater than R-20, you may want to consider building with 2" x 6" framing instead of 2" x 4" framing to allow room for thicker wall cavity insulation—R-19 to R-21.

When shopping for insulation, watch for the National Association of Home Builders (NAHB) certification.

Weatherization

Warm air leaking into your home during the summer and out of your home during the winter can waste a substantial portion of your energy dollars. One of the quickest dollar-saving tasks you can do is caulk, seal, and weatherstrip all seams, cracks, and openings to the outside. You can save 10% or more on your energy bill by reducing the air leaks in your home.

Weatherization Tips

First, test your home for air tightness. On a windy day, hold a lit incense stick next to your windows, doors, electrical boxes, plumbing fixtures, electrical outlets, ceiling fixtures, attic hatches, and other locations where there is a possible air path to the outside. If the smoke stream travels horizontally, you have located an air leak that may need caulking, sealing, or weatherstripping.

- Caulk and weatherstrip doors and windows that leak air.
- Caulk and seal air leaks where plumbing, ducting, or electrical wiring penetrates through exterior walls, floors, ceilings, and soffits over cabinets.
- Install rubber gaskets behind outlet and switch plates on exterior walls.
- Look for dirty spots in your insulation, which often indicate holes where air leaks into and out of your house. You can seal the holes by stapling sheets of plastic over the holes and caulking the edges of the plastic.
- Install storm windows over single-pane windows or replace them with double-pane windows. Storm windows as much as double the R-value of single-pane windows and they

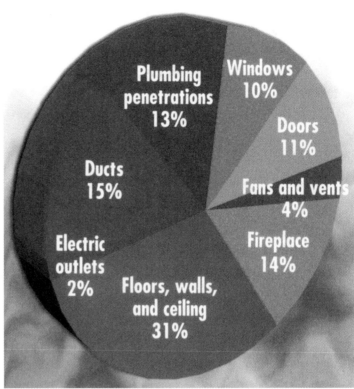

Pie chart:
- Plumbing penetrations 13%
- Windows 10%
- Doors 11%
- Fans and vents 4%
- Fireplace 14%
- Ducts 15%
- Electric outlets 2%
- Floors, walls, and ceiling 31%

How Does the Air Escape?

Air infiltrates in and out of your home through every hole, nook and cranny. About one-third of this air infiltrates through openings in your ceilings, walls, and floors.

can help reduce drafts, water condensation, and frost formation. As a less costly and less permanent alternative, you can use a heavy-duty, clear plastic sheet on a frame or tape clear plastic film to the inside of your window frames during the cold winter months. Remember, the plastic must be sealed tightly to the frame to help reduce infiltration.

- When the fireplace is not in use, keep the flue damper tightly closed. A chimney is designed specifically for smoke to escape, so until you close it, warm air escapes—24 hours a day!
- For new construction, reduce exterior wall leaks by either installing house wrap, taping the joints of exterior sheathing, or comprehensively caulking and sealing the exterior walls.

For more information on insulation, weatherization and ventilation, contact:

Cellulose Insulation Manufacturers Association (CIMA), (937) 222-2462, www.cellulose.org

ENERGY STAR®
(888) STAR-YES; (888-782-7937), www.energystar.gov

Insulation Contractors Association of America (ICAA), (703) 739-0356, www.insulate.org

National Association of Home Builders (NAHB), (800) 368-5242, www.nahb.com

North American Insulation Manufacturers Association (NAIMA), (703) 684-0084, www.naima.org

Owens Corning Customer Service Hotline
(800) GET-PINK; (800-438-7465), www.owenscorning.com

Polyisocyanurate Insulation Manufacturers Association (PIMA), (202) 628-6558, www.pima.org

U.S. Department of Energy's Energy Efficiency and Renewable Energy Clearinghouse (EREC)
(800) DOE-EREC; (800-363-3732), www.eren.doe.gov/erec/factsheets/

Heating and Cooling

Heating and cooling your home uses more energy and drains more energy dollars than any other system in your home. Typically, 44% of your utility bill goes for heating and cooling. What's more, heating and cooling systems in the United States together emit over a half billion tons of carbon dioxide into the atmosphere each year, adding to global warming. They also generate about 24% of the nation's sulfur dioxide and 12% of the nitrogen oxides, the chief ingredients in acid rain.

No matter what kind of heating, ventilation, and air-conditioning system you have in your house, you can save money and increase comfort by properly maintaining and upgrading your equipment. But remember, an energy-efficient furnace alone will not have as great an impact on your energy bills as using the whole-house approach. By combining proper equipment maintenance and upgrades with appropriate insulation, weatherization, and thermostat settings, you can cut your energy bills and your pollution output in half.

Heating and Cooling Tips

- Set your thermostat as low as is comfortable in the winter and as high as is comfortable in the summer.

- Clean or replace filters on furnaces once a month or as needed.

- Clean warm-air registers, baseboard heaters, and radiators as needed; make sure they're not blocked by furniture, carpeting, or drapes.

- Bleed trapped air from hot-water radiators once or twice a season; if in doubt about how to perform this task, call a professional.

- Place heat-resistant radiator reflectors between exterior walls and the radiators.

- Use kitchen, bath, and other ventilating fans wisely; in just one hour, these fans can pull out a houseful of warmed or cooled air. Turn fans off as soon as they have done the job.

- During the heating season, keep the draperies

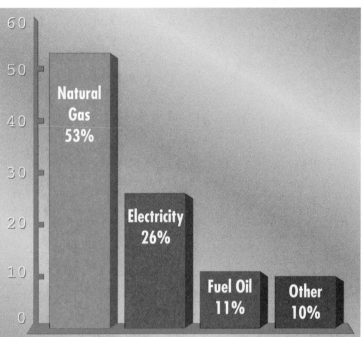

Household Heating Systems

Although there are several different types of fuels available to heat our homes, about half of us use natural gas.

and shades on your south-facing windows open during the day to allow sunlight to enter your home and closed at night to reduce the chill you may feel from cold windows. During the cooling season, keep the window coverings closed during the day to prevent solar gain.

- Close an unoccupied room that is isolated from the rest of the house, such as in a corner, and turn down the thermostat or turn off the heating for that room or zone. However, do not turn the heating off if it adversely affects the rest of your system. For example, if you heat your house with a heat pump, do not close the vents—closing the vents could harm the heat pump.

- Select energy-efficient equipment when you buy new heating and cooling equipment. Your contractor should be able to give you energy fact sheets for different types, models, and designs to help you compare energy usage. Look for high Annual Fuel Utilization Efficiency (AFUE) ratings and the Seasonal Energy Efficiency Ratio (SEER). The national minimums are 78% AFUE and 10 SEER.

- Look for the ENERGY STAR® and EnergyGuide labels. ENERGY STAR® is a program of the U.S. Department of Energy (DOE) and the Environmental Protection Agency (EPA) designed to help consumers identify energy-efficient appliances and products.

Ducts

One of the most important systems in your home, though it's hidden beneath your feet and over your head, may be wasting a lot of your energy dollars. Your home's duct system, a branching network of tubes in the walls, floors, and ceilings, carries the air from your home's furnace and central air conditioner to each room. Ducts are made of sheet metal, fiber glass, or other materials.

Unfortunately, many duct systems are poorly insulated or not insulated properly. Ducts that leak heated air into unheated spaces can add hundreds of dollars a year to your heating and cooling bills. Insulating ducts that are in unconditioned spaces is usually very cost effective. If you are buying a new duct system, consider one that comes with insulation already installed.

What's a Btu?

One Btu, or British thermal unit, is roughly equivalent to burning one kitchen match. That may not sound like much, but a typical home consumes about 100 million Btu per year. Approximately 44% of the total is used for space heating.

Sealing your ducts to prevent leaks is even more important if the ducts are located in an unconditioned area such as an attic or vented crawl space. If the supply ducts are leaking, heated or cooled air can be forced out unsealed joints and lost. In addition, unconditioned air can also be drawn into return ducts through unsealed joints. In the summer, hot attic air can be drawn in, increasing the load on the air conditioner. In the winter, your furnace will have to work longer to keep your house comfortable. Either way, your energy losses cost you money.

Although minor duct repairs are easy to accomplish, ducts in unconditioned spaces should be sealed and insulated by qualified professionals using the appropriate sealing materials. Here are a few simple tips to help with minor duct repairs.

Duct Tips

- Check your ducts for air leaks. First look for sections that should be joined but have separated and then look for obvious holes.

- If you use duct tape to repair and seal your ducts, look for tape with the Underwriters Laboratories (UL) logo to avoid tape that degrades, cracks, and loses its bond with age.

- Remember that insulating ducts in the basement will make the basement colder. If both the ducts and the basement walls are uninsulated, consider insulating both.

- If your basement has been converted to a living area, install both supply and return registers in the basement rooms.

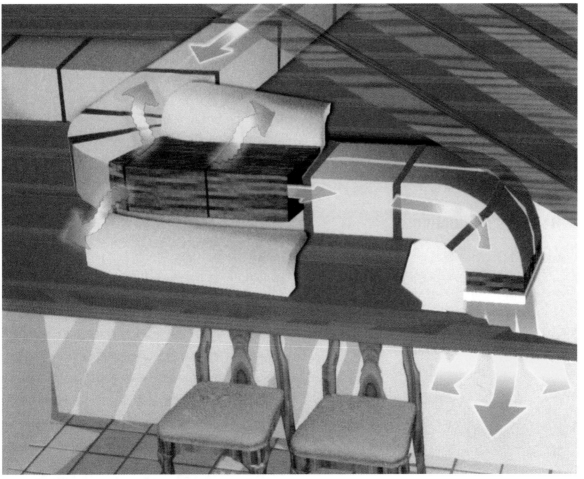

Ducts—Out of Sight, Out of Mind

The unsealed ducts in your attics and crawl spaces lose air—uninsulated ducts lose heat, wasting energy and money.

- Be sure a well-sealed vapor barrier exists on the outside of the insulation on cooling ducts to prevent moisture buildup.

- Get a professional to help you insulate and repair all ducts.

Note: Water pipes and drains in unconditioned spaces could freeze and burst in the space if the heat ducts are fully insulated, because there would be no heat source to prevent the space from freezing in cold weather. However, using an electric heating tape wrap on the pipes can prevent this.

Heat Pumps

If you use electricity to heat your home, consider installing an energy-efficient heat pump system. Heat pumps are the most efficient form of electric heating in moderate climates, providing three times more heating than the equivalent amount of energy they consume in electricity. There are three types of heat pumps: air-to-air, water source, and ground source. They collect heat from the air, water, or ground outside your home and concentrate it for use inside. Heat pumps do double duty as a central air conditioner. They can also cool your home by collecting the heat inside your house and effectively pumping it outside. A heat pump can trim the amount of electricity you use for heating by as much as 30% to 40%.

Look for the ENERGY STAR® label when buying a heat pump.

Heat Pump Tips

- Do not set back the heat pump's thermostat manually if it causes the electric resistance heating to come on. This type of heating, which often is used as a backup to the heat pump, is more expensive.

- Clean or change filters once a month or as needed, and maintain the system according to manufacturer's instructions.

Solar Heating and Cooling

Using passive solar design techniques to heat and cool your home can be both environmentally friendly and cost effective. Passive solar heating techniques include placing larger, insulated windows on south-facing walls and locating thermal mass, such as a concrete slab floor or a heat-absorbing wall, close to the windows. In many cases, you can cut your heating costs by more than 50% compared to the cost of heating the same house that does not include passive solar design.

Passive solar design also can help reduce your cooling costs. Passive solar cooling techniques include carefully designed overhangs, windows with reflective coatings, and the use of reflective coatings on exterior walls and the roof.

However, a passive solar house also requires careful design and site orientation, which depend on the local climate. So, if you are considering passive solar design for new construction or a major remodeling, you should consult an architect familiar with passive solar techniques.

Solar Tips

- Keep all south-facing glass clean.

- Make sure that objects do not block the sunlight shining on concrete slab floors or heat-absorbing walls.

- Consider using insulating curtains to reduce excessive heat loss from large windows at night.

Fireplaces

When you cozy up next to a crackling fire on a cold winter day, you probably don't realize that your fireplace is one of the most inefficient heat sources you can possibly use. It literally sends your energy dollars right up the chimney, along with volumes of warm air. A roaring fire can exhaust as much as 24,000 cubic feet of air per hour to the outside, which must be replaced by cold air coming into the house from the outside. Your heating system must warm up this air, which is then exhausted through your chimney. If you use your conventional fireplace while your central heating system is on, these tips can help reduce energy losses.

Fireplace Tips

- If you never use your fireplace, plug and seal the chimney flue.

- Keep your fireplace damper closed unless a fire is going.

- Keeping the damper open is like keeping a 48-inch window wide open during the winter; it allows warm air to go right up the chimney.

- When you use the fireplace, reduce heat loss by opening dampers in the bottom of the firebox (if provided) or open the nearest window slightly—approximately 1 inch—and close doors leading into the room. Lower the thermostat setting to between 50° and 55°F.

- Install tempered glass doors and a heat-air exchange system that blows warmed air back into the room.

- Check the seal on the flue damper and make it as snug as possible.

- Add caulking around the fireplace hearth.

- Use grates made of C-shaped metal tubes to draw cool room air into the fireplace and circulate warm air back into the room.

The Homeowner's Handbook

Heating and Cooling

Gas and Oil Heating Systems

If you plan to buy a new heating system, ask your local utility or state energy office for information about the latest technologies available to consumers. They can advise you about more efficient systems on the market today. For example, many newer models incorporate designs for burners and heat exchangers that result in higher efficiencies during operation and reduce heat loss when the equipment is off. Check the Shopping Guide under Major Appliances for additional information on how to understand heating system ratings.

Look for the ENERGY STAR® and EnergyGuide labels.

Air Conditioners

It might surprise you to know that buying a bigger room air-conditioning unit won't necessarily make you feel more comfortable during the hot summer months. In fact, a room air conditioner that's too big for the area it is supposed to cool will perform less efficiently and less effectively than a smaller, properly sized unit. This is because room units work better if they run for relatively long periods of time than if they are continually switching off and on. Longer run times allow air conditioners to maintain a more constant room temperature.

Sizing is equally important for central air-conditioning systems, which need to be sized by professionals. If you have a central air system in your home, set the fan to shut off at the same time as the cooling unit (compressor). In other words, don't use the system's central fan to provide circulation, but instead use circulating fans in individual rooms.

The shopping guide in the back of this booklet will help you find the right size unit for your needs. Look for the ENERGY STAR® and EnergyGuide labels.

Cooling Tips

- Whole-house fans help cool your home by pulling cool air through the house and exhausting warm air through the attic. They are effective when operated at night and when the outside air is cooler than the inside.

- Set your thermostat as high as comfortably possible in the summer. The less difference between the indoor and outdoor temperatures, the lower your overall cooling bill will be.

- Don't set your thermostat at a colder setting than normal when you turn on your air conditioner. It will not cool your home any faster and could result in excessive cooling and, therefore, unnecessary expense.

- Consider using an interior fan in conjunction with your window air conditioner to spread the cooled air more effectively through your home without greatly increasing your power use.

- Don't place lamps or TV sets near your air-conditioning thermostat. The thermostat senses heat from these appliances, which can cause the air conditioner to run longer than necessary.

- Plant trees or shrubs to shade air-conditioning units but not to block the airflow. A unit operating in the shade uses as much as 10% less electricity than the same one operating in the sun.

Heating and Cooling

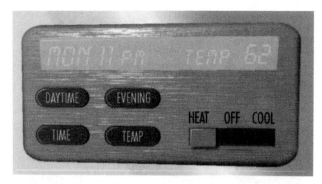

Nighttime Heating

Using a programmable thermostat, you can automatically turn down your heat at night or when you are not at home.

Nighttime Cooling

In the summer, you can save money by automatically turning your air conditioning up at night.

Programmable Thermostats

You can save as much as 10% a year on your heating and cooling bills by simply turning your thermostat back 10% to 15% for 8 hours. You can do this automatically without sacrificing comfort by installing an automatic setback or programmable thermostat.

Using a programmable thermostat, you can adjust the times you turn on the heating or air-conditioning according to a pre-set schedule. As a result, you don't operate the equipment as much when you are asleep or when the house or part of the house is not occupied. (These thermostats are not meant to be used with heat pumps.) Programmable thermostats can store and repeat multiple daily settings (six or more temperature settings a day) that you can manually override without affecting the rest of the daily or weekly program. When shopping for a programmable thermostat, be sure to look for the ENERGY STAR® label.

For more information on heating and cooling, contact:

Air Conditioning and Refrigeration Institute (ACRI), (703) 524-8800, www.ari.org

ENERGY STAR®
(888) STAR-YES; (888-782-7937),
www.energystar.gov

Gas Appliance Manufacturers Association
(703) 525-9565, www.gamanet.org

Owens Corning Customer Service Hotline
(800) GET-PINK; (800-438-7465),
www.owenscorning.com

U.S. Department of Energy's Energy Efficiency and Renewable Energy Clearinghouse (EREC)
(800) DOE-EREC; (800-363-3732),
www.eren.doe.gov/erec/factsheets

Water Heating

Water heating is the third largest energy expense in your home. It typically accounts for about 14% of your utility bill.

There are four ways to cut your water heating bills: use less hot water, turn down the thermostat on your water heater, insulate your water heater, and buy a new, more efficient water heater. A family of four, each showering for 5 minutes a day, uses 700 gallons of water a week; this is enough for a 3-year supply of drinking water for one person. You can cut that amount in half simply by using low-flow nonaerating showerheads and faucets.

Water Heating Tips

• Repair leaky faucets promptly; a leaky faucet wastes gallons of water in a short period.

• Insulate your electric hot-water storage tank and pipes, but be careful not to cover the thermostat.

• Insulate your gas or oil hot-water storage tank and pipes, but be careful not to cover the water heater's top, bottom, thermostat, or burner compartment; when in doubt, get professional help.

• Install nonaerating low-flow faucets and showerheads.

• Buy a new water heater. While it may cost more initially than a standard water heater, the energy savings will continue during the lifetime of the appliance.

• Although most water heaters last 10-15 years, it's best to start shopping for a new one if yours is more than 7 years old. Doing some research before your heater fails will enable you to select one that most appropriately meets your needs.

• Lower the thermostat on your water heater; water heaters sometimes come from the factory with high temperature settings, but a setting of 115°F provides comfortable hot water for most uses.

• Drain a quart of water from your water tank every 3 months to remove sediment that impedes heat transfer and lowers the efficiency of your heater. The type of water tank you have determines the steps to take, so follow the manufacturer's advice.

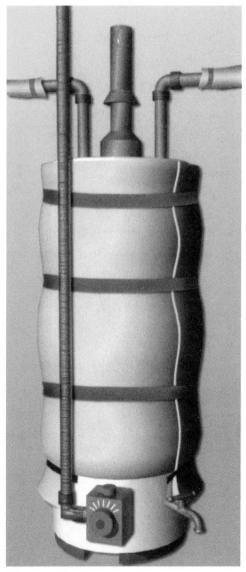

Water Heater

Insulate your water heater to save energy and money.

• If you heat with electricity and live in a warm and sunny climate, consider installing a solar water heater. The solar units are environmentally friendly and can now be installed on your roof to blend with the architecture of your house.

• Take more showers than baths. Bathing uses the most hot water in the average household. You use 15-25 gallons of hot water for a bath, but less than 10 gallons during a 5-minute shower.

• Consider the installation of a drain water waste heat recovery system.

• Look for the FTC EnergyGuide label.

Solar Water Heaters

If you heat with electricity and you have an unshaded, south-facing location (such as a roof) on your property, consider installing a solar water heater. More than 1.5 million homes and businesses in the United States have invested in solar water heating systems and over 94% of these customers consider the systems a good investment. Solar water heating systems also are good for the environment. Solar water heaters avoid the harmful greenhouse gas emissions associated with electricity production. During a 20-year period, one solar water heater can avoid over 50 tons of carbon dioxide emissions.

When shopping for a solar water heater, watch for systems certified by the Solar Rating and Certification Corporation (SRCC) or the Florida Solar Energy Center (FSEC).

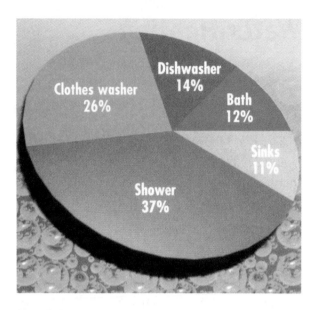

Hot Water Usage (based on national averages)
The typical U.S. homeowner's water consumption by place of use.

For more information on how you can save money on your water heating bill, contact:

American Solar Energy Society (ASES)
(303) 443-3130, www.ASES.org/solar

Florida Solar Energy Center (FSEC)
(407) 638-1015, www.fsec.ucf.edu

Gas Appliance Manufacturers Association
(703) 525-9565, www.gamanet.org

Owens Corning Customer Service Hotline
(800) GET-PINK; (800-438-7465),
www.owenscorning.com

Solar Energy Industries Association (SEIA)
(703) 248-0702, www.seia.com

Solar Rating and Certification Corporation (SRCC), (407) 638-1537

U.S. Department of Energy's Energy Efficiency and Renewable Energy Clearinghouse (EREC)
(800) DOE-EREC; (800-363-3732),
www.eren.doe.gov/erec/factsheets

Windows

Windows can be one of your home's most attractive features. Windows provide views, daylighting, ventilation, and solar heating in the winter. Unfortunately, they also can account for 10% to 25% of your heating bill. During the summer, sunny windows make your air conditioner work two to three times harder. If you live in the Sun Belt, look into new solar control spectrally selective windows, which can cut the cooling load by more than half.

If your home has single-pane windows, as almost half of U.S. homes do, consider replacing them. New double-pane windows with high-performance glass (e.g., low-e or spectrally selective) are available on the market. In colder climates, select windows that are gas filled with low-emissivity (low-e) coatings on the glass to reduce heat loss. In warmer climates, select windows with spectrally selective coatings to reduce heat gain. If you are building a new home, you can offset some of the cost of installing more efficient windows because doing so allows you to buy smaller, less expensive heating and cooling equipment.

If you decide not to replace your windows, the simpler, less costly measures listed below can improve the performance of your windows.

Warm-Climate Windows

In the summertime, the sun shining through your windows heats up the room. Windows with spectrally selective coatings on the glass reflect some of the sunlight, keeping your rooms cooler.

Cold-Climate Window Tips

• Install exterior or interior storm windows; storm windows can reduce your heat loss through the windows by 25% to 50%. Storm windows should have weatherstripping at all moveable joints; be made of strong, durable materials; and have interlocking or overlapping joints. Low-e storm windows save even more energy.

• Repair and weatherize your current storm windows, if necessary.

• Install tight-fitting, insulating window shades on windows that feel drafty after weatherizing.

• Close your curtains and shades at night; open them during the day.

• Keep windows on the south side of your house clean to maximize solar gain.

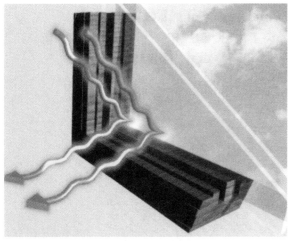

Cold-Climate Windows

Double-pane windows with low-e coating on the glass reflect heat back into the room during the winter months.

Warm-Climate Window Tips

• Install white window shades, drapes, or blinds to reflect heat away from the house.

• Close curtains on south- and west-facing windows during the day.

• Install awnings on south- and west-facing windows.

• Apply sun-control or other reflective films on south-facing windows to reduce solar gain.

Buying New Windows

New windows are long-term investments that have a large impact on your home's energy systems. Today, there are many new window technologies available that are worth considering, especially those with the ENERGY STAR® label. Glazing materials now come with a variety of selective coatings and other features; frames are available in aluminum, wood, vinyl, fiber glass, or combinations of these materials. Each type of glazing material and frame has advantages and disadvantages.

Shopping Tips

• When you're shopping for new windows, look for the National Fenestration Rating Council (NFRC) label; it means the window's performance is certified.

• Remember, the lower the U-value, the better the insulation. In colder climates, a U-value of 0.35 or below is recommended. These windows have at least double glazing and low-e coating.

• In warm climates, where summertime heat gain is the main concern, look for windows with double glazing and spectrally selective coatings that reduce heat gain.

• Select windows with air leakage ratings of 0.3 cubic feet per minute or less.

• In temperate climates with both heating and cooling seasons, select windows with both low U-values and low solar heat gain coefficiency (SHGC) to maximize energy benefits.

• Look for the ENERGY STAR® and EnergyGuide labels

For more information about windows, contact:

American Architectural Manufacturers Association (AAMA), (847) 303-5664, www.aamanet.org

Efficient Windows Collaborative
(202) 857-0666, www.efficientwindows.org

ENERGY STAR®
(888) STAR-YES; (888-782-7937)
www.energystar.gov

National Fenestration Rating Council (NFRC)
(301) 589-6372, www.nfrc.org

National Wood Window and Door Association
(800) 223-2301, www.nwwda.org

Owens Corning Customer Service Hotline
(800) GET-PINK; (800-438-7465),
www.owenscorning.com

U.S. Department of Energy's Energy Efficiency and Renewable Energy Clearinghouse (EREC)
(800) DOE-EREC; (800-363-3732),
www.eren.doe.gov/erec/factsheets

Landscaping

Landscaping is a natural and beautiful way to keep your home more comfortable and reduce your energy bills. In addition to adding aesthetic value and environmental quality to your home, a well-placed tree, shrub, or vine can deliver effective shade, act as a windbreak, and reduce overall energy bills.

Carefully positioned trees can save up to 25% of a typical household's energy for heating and cooling. Computer models from DOE predict that just three trees, properly placed around the house, can save an average household between $100 and $250 in heating and cooling energy costs annually. During the summer months, the most effective way to keep your home cool is to prevent the heat from building up in the first place. A primary source of heat buildup is sunlight absorbed by your home's roof, walls, and windows. Dark-colored home exteriors absorb 70% to 90% of the radiant energy from the sun that strikes the home's surfaces. Some of this absorbed energy is then transferred into your home by way of conduction, resulting in heat gain inside the house. In contrast, light-colored surfaces effectively reflect most of the heat away from your home. Landscaping also can help block and absorb the sun's energy to help decrease heat buildup in your home by providing shade and evaporative cooling.

Shading and evaporative cooling from trees can reduce the air temperature around your home. Studies conducted by the Lawrence Berkeley National Laboratory found summer daytime air temperatures to be 3° to 6°F cooler in tree-shaded neighborhoods than in treeless areas. The energy-conserving landscape strategies you should use for your home depend on the type of climate in which you live.

Landscaping Tips—Dependent on Geographic Area

- Trees that lose their leaves in the fall (i.e., deciduous) are the most effective at reducing heating and cooling energy costs. When selectively placed around a house, they provide excellent protection from the summer sun but permit winter sunlight to reach and warm your house. The height, growth rate, branch spread, and shape are all factors to consider in choosing a tree.

Buildings and Trees—Natural Partners

Deciduous trees planted on the south and on the west sides will keep your house cool in the summer and allow sun to shine in the windows in the winter.

- Vines provide shading and cooling. Grown on trellises, vines can shade windows or the whole side of a house.

- Deflect winter winds by planting evergreen trees and shrubs on the north and west sides of your house; deflect summer winds by planting on the south and west sides of your house.

Orientation of the house and surrounding landscaping has a large effect on energy consumption. A well-oriented, well-designed home admits low-angle winter sun to reduce heating bills; rejects overhead summer sun to reduce cooling bills; and minimizes the chill effect of winter winds. Fences, walls, other nearby buildings, and rows of trees or shrubs block or channel the wind. Bodies of water moderate temperature but increase humidity and produce glare. Trees provide shade, windbreaks, and wind channels. Pavement reflects or absorbs heat, depending on whether it is light or dark in color.

Contact your county extension agents, public libraries, local nurseries, landscape architects, landscape contractors, and state and local energy offices for additional information on energy-efficient landscaping and regional plants and their maintenance requirements.

White Roofs

Just as wearing white clothes reflects the sun's heat from your body, a white or light-colored roof will help reflect the sun's heat away from your home. This strategy works particularly well when trees are located next to the reflecting surface. Not only does the tree provide shade, it absorbs the reflected sunlight for photosynthesis. In the process, water evaporates from the tree, cooling the air around the house.

For more information on landscaping for energy efficiency, contact:

American Society of Landscape Architects (ASLA), (202) 898-2444, www.asla.org

National Arbor Day Foundation (NADF)
(402) 474-5655, www.arborday.org

U.S. Department of Agriculture
County Extension Service - Local Chapter

U.S. Department of Energy's
Energy Efficiency and Renewable Energy Clearinghouse (EREC)
(800) DOE-EREC; (363-3732),
www.eren.doe.gov/erec/factsheets

Lighting

Increasing your lighting efficiency is one of the fastest ways to decrease your energy bills. If you replace 25% of your lights in high-use areas with fluorescents, you can save about 50% of your lighting energy bill.

Indoor Lighting

Use linear fluorescent and energy-efficient compact fluorescent lamps (CFLs) in fixtures throughout your home to provide high-quality and high-efficiency lighting. Fluorescent lamps are much more efficient than incandescent bulbs and last 6 to 10 times longer. Although fluorescent and compact fluorescent lamps are more expensive than incandescent bulbs, they pay for themselves by saving energy over their lifetime. Look for the ENERGY STAR® label when purchasing these products. The Pacific Northwest National Laboratory has also compiled a list of suppliers for sub-compact fluorescent lamps.

Indoor Lighting Tips

- Turn off the lights in any room you're not using, or consider installing timers, photo cells, or occupancy sensors to reduce the amount of time your lights are on.

- Use task lighting; instead of brightly lighting an entire room, focus the light where you need it. For example, use fluorescent under-cabinet lighting for kitchen sinks and countertops under cabinets.

- Consider three-way lamps; they make it easier to keep lighting levels low when brighter light is not necessary.

- Use 4-foot fluorescent fixtures with reflective backing and electronic ballasts for your workroom, garage, and laundry areas.

- Consider using 4-watt mini-fluorescent or electro-luminescent night lights. Both lights are much more efficient than their incandescent counterparts. The luminescent lights are cool to the touch.

Outdoor Lighting

Many homeowners use outdoor lighting for decoration and security. When shopping for outdoor lights, you will find a variety of products, from low-voltage pathway lighting to high-sodium motion-detector floodlights. Some stores also carry lights powered by small photovoltaic (PV) modules that convert sunlight directly into electricity; consider PV-powered lights for areas that are not close to an existing power supply line.

Compact Fluorescent Bulbs

These compact fluorescent lamps are four times more energy efficient than incandescent lamps and provide the same lighting.

Outdoor Lighting Tips

• Use outdoor lights with a photocell unit or a timer so they will turn off during the day.

• Turn off decorative outdoor gas lamps; just eight gas lamps burning year round use as much natural gas as it takes to heat an average-size home during an entire winter.

• Exterior lighting is one of the best places to use CFLs because of their long life. If you live in a cold climate, be sure to buy a lamp with a cold-weather ballast.

For more information on energy-efficient lighting, contact:

ENERGY STAR®
(888) STAR-YES; (888-782-7937),
www.energystar.gov

**U.S. Department of Energy's
Energy Efficiency and Renewable Energy
Clearinghouse (EREC)**
(800) DOE-EREC; (800-363-3732),
www.eren.doe.gov/erec/factsheets

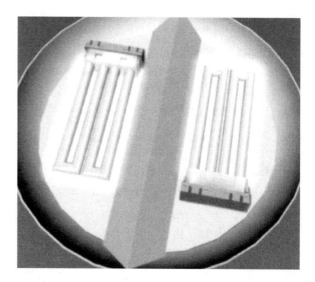

Torchiere Lamp

Halogen lamps generate excessive heat that can create fire hazards. Use compact fluorescent lamps in your torchiere fixtures. They are safer and use much less energy.

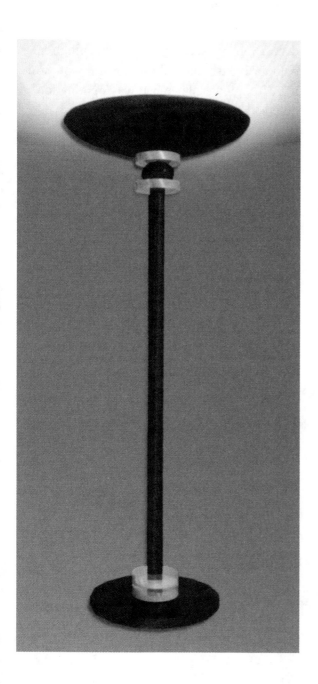

Appliances

Appliances account for about 20% of your household's energy consumption, with refrigerators and clothes dryers at the top of the consumption list.

What's the Real Cost?

Every appliance has two price tags—a purchase price and the operating cost.

When you're shopping for appliances, you can think of two price tags. The first one covers the purchase price—think of it as a down payment. The second price tag is the cost of operating the appliance during its lifetime. You'll be paying on that second price tag every month with your utility bill for the next 10 to 20 years, depending on the appliance. Refrigerators last an average of 20 years; room air conditioners and dishwashers, about 10 years each; clothes washers, about 14 years.

What's a kilowatt?

When you cook a pot of rice for 1 hour, you use 1000 watt hours of electricity! One thousand watt hours equals 1 kilowatt-hour, or 1kWh. Your utility bill usually shows what you are charged for the kilowatt-hours you use. The average residential rate is 8.3 cents per kWh. A typical U.S. household consumes about 10,000 kWh per year, costing an average of $830 annually.

When you do have to shop for a new appliance, look for the ENERGY STAR® label. ENERGY STAR® appliances have been identified by the U.S. Environmental Protection Agency and DOE as being the most energy-efficient products in their classes. They usually exceed minimum federal standards by a substantial amount. The appliance shopping guide lists some of the major appliances that carry the ENERGY STAR® label and provides helpful information on what to look for when shopping for an appliance.

To help you figure out whether an appliance is energy efficient, the federal government requires most appliances to display the bright yellow and black EnergyGuide label. Although these labels will not tell you which appliance is the most efficient, they will tell you the annual energy consumption and operating cost for each appliance so you can compare them yourself.

Dishwashers

Most of the energy used by a dishwasher is for water heating. The EnergyGuide label estimates how much power is needed per year to run the appliance and to heat the water based on the yearly cost of gas and electric water heating.

Dishwasher Tips

- Check the manual that came with your dishwasher for the manufacturer's recommendations on water temperature; many have internal heating elements that allow you to set the water heater to a lower temperature.

- Scrape, don't rinse, off large food pieces and bones. Soaking or prewashing is generally only recommended in cases of burned-on or dried-on food.

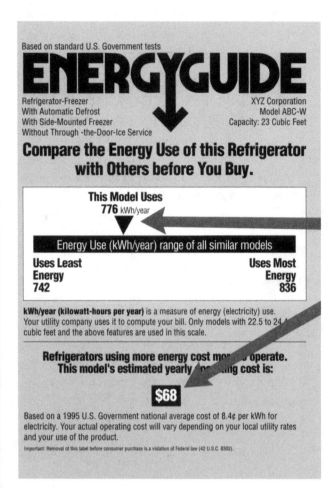

Based on standard U.S. Government tests

ENERGYGUIDE

Refrigerator-Freezer
With Automatic Defrost
With Side-Mounted Freezer
Without Through -the-Door-Ice Service

XYZ Corporation
Model ABC-W
Capacity: 23 Cubic Feet

Compare the Energy Use of this Refrigerator with Others before You Buy.

This Model Uses
776 kWh/year

Energy Use (kWh/year) range of all similar models

Uses Least Energy 742

Uses Most Energy 836

kWh/year (kilowatt-hours per year) is a measure of energy (electricity) use. Your utility company uses it to compute your bill. Only models with 22.5 to 24.4 cubic feet and the above features are used in this scale.

Refrigerators using more energy cost more to operate. This model's estimated yearly operating cost is:

$68

Based on a 1995 U.S. Government national average cost of 8.4¢ per kWh for electricity. Your actual operating cost will vary depending on your local utility rates and your use of the product.

Important: Removal of this label before consumer purchase is a violation of Federal law (42 U.S.C. 8302).

How to Read the EnergyGuide Label

The EnergyGuide label gives you two important pieces of information you can use for comparison of different brands and models when shopping for a new refrigerator:

- Estimated energy consumption on a scale showing a range for similar models

- Estimated yearly operating cost based on the national average cost of electricity.

Refrigerators

The EnergyGuide label on new refrigerators will tell you how much electricity in kilowatt-hours (kWh) a particular model uses in one year. The smaller the number, the less energy the refrigerator uses and the less it will cost you to operate. In addition to the EnergyGuide label, don't forget to look for the ENERGY STAR® label. A new refrigerator with an ENERGY STAR® label will save you between $35 and $70 a year compared to the models designed 15 years ago. This adds up to between $525 and $1,050 during the average 15-year life of the unit.

Refrigerator/Freezer Energy Tips

- Look for a refrigerator with automatic moisture control. Models with this feature have been engineered to prevent moisture accumulation on the cabinet exterior without the addition of a heater. This is not the same thing as an "anti-sweat" heater. Models with an anti-sweat heater will consume 5% to 10% more energy than models without this feature.

- Be sure your dishwasher is full, but not overloaded.

- Don't use the "rinse hold" on your machine for just a few soiled dishes. It uses 3 to 7 gallons of hot water each time you use it.

- Let your dishes air dry; if you don't have an automatic air-dry switch, turn off the control knob after the final rinse and prop the door open a little so the dishes will dry faster.

- When shopping for a new dishwasher, look for the ENERGY STAR® label. ENERGY STAR® dishwashers use less water and energy and must exceed minimum federal standards by at least 13%.

- Don't keep your refrigerator or freezer too cold. Recommended temperatures are 37° to 40°F for the fresh food compartment of the refrigerator and 5°F for the freezer section. If you have a separate freezer for long-term storage, it should be kept at 0°F.

- To check refrigerator temperature, place an appliance thermometer in a glass of water in the center of the refrigerator. Read it after 24 hours. To check the freezer temperature, place a thermometer between frozen packages. Read it after 24 hours.

- Regularly defrost manual-defrost refrigerators and freezers; frost buildup increases the amount of energy needed to keep the motor running. Don't allow frost to build up more than one-quarter of an inch.

- Make sure your refrigerator door seals are airtight. Test them by closing the door over a piece of paper or a dollar bill so it is half in and half out of the refrigerator. If you can pull the paper or bill out easily, the latch may need adjustment or the seal may need replacing.

- Cover liquids and wrap foods stored in the refrigerator. Uncovered foods release moisture and make the compressor work harder.

- Move your refrigerator out from the wall and vacuum its condenser coils once a year unless you have a no-clean condenser model. Your refrigerator will run for shorter periods with clean coils.

Other Energy-Saving Kitchen Tips

- Be sure to place the faucet lever on the kitchen sink in the cold position when using small amounts of water; placing the lever in the hot position uses energy to heat the water even though it never reaches the faucet.

- If you need to purchase a gas oven or range, look for one with an automatic, electric ignition system. An electric ignition saves gas—because a pilot light is not burning continuously.

- In gas appliances, look for blue flames; yellow flames indicate the gas is burning inefficiently and an adjustment may be needed. Consult your manufacturer or your local utility.

- Keep range-top burners and reflectors clean; they will reflect the heat better, and you will save energy.

- Use a covered kettle or pan to boil water; it's faster and it uses less energy.

- Match the size of the pan to the heating element.

Refrigerator Choices

Refrigerators with the freezer on top are more efficient than those with freezers on the side.

- If you cook with electricity, turn the stovetop burners off several minutes before the allotted cooking time. The heating element will stay hot long enough to finish the cooking without using more electricity. The same principle applies to oven cooking.

- Use small electric pans or toaster ovens for small meals rather than your large stove or oven. A toaster oven uses a third to half as much energy as a full-sized oven.

- Use pressure cookers and microwave ovens whenever it is convenient to do so. They can save energy by significantly reducing cooking time.

Laundry

About 80% to 85% of the energy used for washing clothes is for heating the water. There are two ways to reduce the amount of energy used for washing clothes—use less water and use cooler water. Unless you're dealing with oily stains, the warm or cold water setting on your machine will generally do a good job of cleaning your clothes. Switching your temperature setting from hot to warm can cut a load's energy use in half.

When shopping for a new washer, look for an ENERGY STAR® machine. These machines may cost more to buy but they use about a third of the energy and less water than typical machines. You'll also save more on

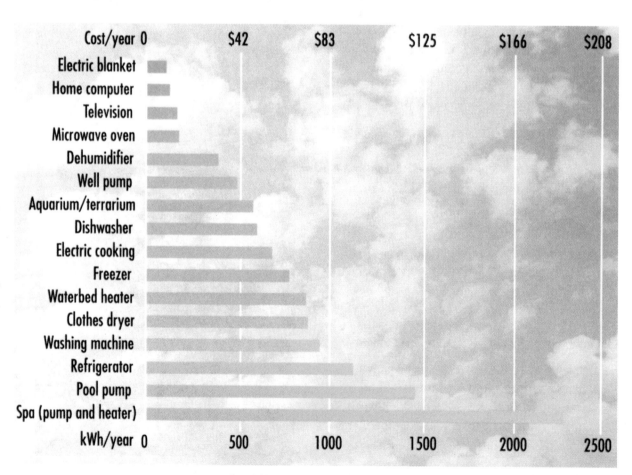

How Much Electricity Do Appliances Use?

This chart shows how much energy a typical appliance uses per year and its corresponding cost based on national averages. For example, a refrigerator uses almost five times the electricity the average television uses.

The Homeowner's Handbook

clothes drying, because most remove more water from your clothes during the spin cycle. Look for the ENERGY STAR® label.

When shopping for a new clothes dryer, look for one with a moisture sensor that automatically shuts off the machine when your clothes are dry. Not only will this save energy, it will save wear and tear on your clothes caused by over-drying. Keep in mind that gas dryers are less expensive to operate than electric dryers. The cost of drying a typical load of laundry in an electric dryer is 30 to 40 cents compared to 15 to 25 cents in a gas dryer.

Laundry Tips

- Wash your clothes in cold water using cold-water detergents whenever possible.

- Wash and dry full loads. If you are washing a small load, use the appropriate water-level setting.

- Dry towels and heavier cottons in a separate load from lighter-weight clothes.

- Don't over-dry your clothes. If your machine has a moisture sensor, use it.

- Clean the lint filter in the dryer after every load to improve air circulation.

- Use the cool-down cycle to allow the clothes to finish drying with the residual heat in the dryer.

- Periodically inspect your dryer vent to ensure it is not blocked. This will save energy and may prevent a fire. Manufacturers recommend using rigid venting material, not plastic vents that may collapse and cause blockages.

- Look for the ENERGY STAR® and EnergyGuide labels.

For more information on energy-efficient appliances, contact:

Association of Home Appliance Manufacturers, (202) 872-5955, www.aham.org

ENERGY STAR®
(888) STAR-YES; (888-782-7937), www.energystar.gov

U.S. Department of Energy's Energy Efficiency and Renewable Energy Clearinghouse (EREC)
(800) DOE-EREC; (800-363-3732), www.eren.doe.gov/erec/factsheets

Major Appliance Shopping Guide

This easy-to-read guide may help you understand how appliances are rated for efficiency, what the ratings mean, and what to look for while shopping for new appliances.

Appliances	Rating	Special Considerations
Natural Gas and Oil Systems	Look for the **FTC** (Federal Trade Commission) EnergyGuide label with an **AFUE** (Annual Fuel Utilization Efficiency) rating for gas- and oil-fired furnaces and boilers. The AFUE measures the seasonal or annual efficiency. ENERGY STAR® furnaces have a 90 AFUE or greater.	Bigger is not always better! Too large a system costs more and operates inefficiently. Have a professional assess your needs and recommend the type and size of system you should purchase.
Air-Source Heat Pumps 	Look for the EnergyGuide label that contains the **SEER** (Seasonal Energy Efficiency Ratio) and **HSPF** (Heating Seasonal Performance Factor) for heat pumps. The SEER measures the energy efficiency during the cooling season and HSPF measures the efficiency during the heating season. The ENERGY STAR® minimum efficiency level is 12 SEER or higher.	If you live in a cool climate, look for a heat pump with a high HSPF. If you purchase an ENERGY STAR® heat pump, you are getting a product that is in the top 25% for efficiency. Contact a professional for advice on purchasing a heat pump.
Central Air Conditioners 	Look for the EnergyGuide label with a **SEER** (Seasonal Energy Efficiency Rating) for central air conditioners. The ENERGY STAR® minimum efficiency level is 12 SEER. ENERGY STAR® central air conditioners exceed federal standards by at least 20%.	Air conditioners that bear the ENERGY STAR® label may be twice as efficient as some existing systems. Contact a professional for advice on sizing a central air system.

Room Air Conditioners

Look for the EnergyGuide label with an **EER** (Energy Efficiency Rating) for room air conditioners. The higher the EER, the more efficient the unit is. ENERGY STAR® units are among the most energy-efficient products.

What size to buy?

Area in square feet	btu/hour
100 to 150	5,000
150 to 250	6,000
250 to 350	7,000
350 to 400	9,000
400 to 450	10,000
450 to 550	12,000
550 to 700	14,000
700 to 1,000	18,000

Two major decisions should guide your purchase. Buy a correctly sized unit. Buy an energy-efficient unit. If the room is very sunny, increase capacity by 10%. If the unit is for a kitchen, increase the capacity by 4,000 Btu per hour.

The ENERGY STAR® label is the government's seal of approval. It was created by the U.S. Department of Energy and the U.S. Environmental Protection Agency. These agencies set the criteria to help shoppers for large and small home appliances identify the most energy-efficient products on the market. ENERGY STAR®-labeled appliances exceed existing federal efficiency standards, typically, by 13% to 20%, and as much as 110% for some appliances. Customers can be assured that the appliance being purchased is a high-performance product which will reduce the operating cost of that appliance or product every month during the course of its lifetime.

Appliances	Rating	Special Considerations
Programmable Thermostats	For minimum ENERGY STAR® efficiency, thermostats should have at least two programs, four temperature settings each, a hold feature that allows users to temporarily override settings, and the ability to maintain room temperature with 2°F of desired temperature.	Look for a thermostat that allows you to easily use two separate programs; an "advanced recovery" feature that can be programmed to reach the desired temperature at a specific time; a hold feature that temporarily overrides the setting without deleting preset programs; and the ENERGY STAR® label.
Water Heaters	Look for the EnergyGuide label that tells how much energy the water heater uses in one year. Also, look for the **FHR** (First Hour Rating) of the water heater, which measures the maximum hot water the heater will deliver in the first hour of use.	If you typically need a lot of hot water at once, the FHR will be important to you. Sizing is important—call your local utility for advice.
Windows	Look for the **NFRC** (National Fenestration Rating Council) label that provides U-values and **SHGC** (solar heat gain coefficient) values. The lower the U-value, the better the insulation.	Look at the Climate Region Map on the ENERGY STAR® label to be sure that the window, door, or skylight you have selected is appropriate for where you live.
Refrigerators and Freezers 	Look for the EnergyGuide label that tells how much electricity, in kilowatt-hours (kWh), the refrigerator or freezer will use in one year. The smaller the number, the less energy it uses. ENERGY STAR® labeled units exceed federal standards by at least 20%.	Look for energy-efficient refrigerators and freezers. Refrigerators with freezers on top are more efficient than those with freezers on the side. Also look for heavy door hinges that create a good door seal.
Dishwashers 	Look for the EnergyGuide label that tells how much electricity, in kilowatt-hours (kWh), the dishwasher will use in one year. The smaller the number, the less energy it uses. ENERGY STAR® dishwashers exceed federal standards by at least 13%.	Look for features that will reduce water use, such as booster heaters and smart controls. Ask how many gallons of water the dishwasher uses during different cycles. Dishwashers that use the least amount of water will cost the least to operate.
Clothes Washers 	Look for the EnergyGuide label that tells how much electricity, in kilowatt-hours (kWh), the clothes washer will use in one year. The smaller the number, the less energy it uses. ENERGY STAR® clothes washer uses less than 50% of the energy used by standard washers.	Look for the following design features that help clothes washers cut water usage: water level controls, "suds-saver" features, spin cycle adjustment, and large capacity. For double the efficiency, buy an ENERGY STAR® unit.

Major Appliance Shopping Guide

Source List

Air Conditioning and Refrigeration Institute
4301 North Fairfax Drive, Suite 425
Arlington, VA 22203
E-mail: ari@ari.org
Phone: (703) 524-8800
Fax: (703) 528-3816

Alliance to Save Energy
1200 18th Street, NW
Suite 900
Washington, DC 20036
E-mail: info@ase.org
Phone: (202) 857-0666
Fax: (202) 331-9588

American Architectural Manufacturers Association
(AAMA)
1827 Walden Office Square, Suite 104
Schaumburg, IL 60173-4628
E-mail: webmaster@AAMANET.org
Phone: (847) 303-5664
Fax: (847) 303-5774

American Council for an Energy-Efficient
Economy (ACEEE)
1001 Connecticut Avenue Suite 801
Washington, D.C. 20036
Phone (Research and Conferences):
(202) 429-8873
Publications: (202) 429-0063

American Society of Landscape
Architects (ASLA)
636 Eye Street, NW
Washington, DC 20001-3736
Phone: (202) 898-2444
Fax: (202) 898-1185

American Solar Energy Society (ASES)
2400 Central Avenue, Unit G-1
Boulder, CO 80301
E-mail: ases@ases.org
Phone: (303) 443-3130
Fax: (303) 443-3212

Association of Home Appliance Manufacturers
1111 19th Street, NW
Suite 402
Washington, DC 20036
E-mail: aham@aham.org
Phone: (202) 872-5955
Fax: (202) 872-9354

Cellulose Insulation Manufacturers Association
(CIMA)
136 South Keowee Street
Dayton, OH 45402
E-mail: CIMA@dayton.net
Phone: (937) 222-2462
Fax: (937) 222-5794

Energy Star®
Environmental Protection Agency (EPA)
401 M Street, SW, (6202J)
Washington, DC 20460
Phone: (202) 564-9190
Toll Free: (888) STAR-YES; (888-782-7937)
Fax: (202) 564-9569
Fax-back system: (202) 233-9659

Federal Trade Commission
Bureau of Consumer Protection
CRC-240
Washington, DC 20580
Phone: (202) FTC-HELP (202-382-4357)

Florida Solar Energy Center (FSEC)
1679 Clearlake Road
Cocoa, FL 32922-5703
E-mail: webmaster@fsec.ucf.edu
Phone: (407) 638-1015
Fax: (407) 638-1010

Gas Appliance Manufacturers Association
1901 North Moore Street, Suite 1100
Arlington, VA 22209
E-mail: information@gamanet.org
Phone: (703) 525-9565
Fax: (703) 525-0718

Insulation Contractors Association of America
(ICAA)
1321 Duke Street, Suite 303
Alexandria, VA 22314
E-mail: icaa@insulate.org
Phone: (703) 739-0356
Fax: (703) 739-0412

National Arbor Day Foundation (NADF)
100 Arbor Avenue
Nebraska City, NE 68410
Phone: (402) 474-5655

National Association of Home Builders (NAHB)
1201 15th Street, NW
Washington, DC 20005
E-mail: info@nahb.com
Phone: (800) 368-5242

National Association of State Energy Officials
    (NASEO)
1414 Prince Street, Suite 200
Alexandria, VA 22314
E-mail: info@naseo.org
Phone: (703) 299-8800
Fax: (703) 299-6208

National Fenestration Rating Council (NFRC)
1300 Spring Street, Suite 500
Silver Spring, MD 20910
E-mail: NFRCUSA@aol.com
Phone: (301) 589-NFRC (301-589-6372)
Fax: (301) 588-0854

National Insulation Association
99 Canal Center Plaza, Suite 222
Alexandria, VA 22314-1538
E-mail: niainfo@insulation.org
Phone: (703) 683-6422
Fax: (703) 549-4838

National Wood Window and Door Association
1400 East Touhy Avenue, Suite 470
Des Plaines, IL 60018
E-mail: admin@wdma.com
Phone: (800) 223-2301
Fax: (847) 299-1286

North American Insulation Manufacturers Association
    (NAIMA)
44 Canal Center Plaza, Suite 310
Alexandria, VA 22314
E-mail: insulation@naima.org
Phone: (703) 684-0084
Fax: (703) 684-0427

Owens Corning
One Owens Corning Parkway
Toledo, OH 43659
Phone: (419) 248-8000
Customer Service Hotline:
(800) GET PINK (800-438-7465)

Polyisocyanurate Insulation Manufacturers
    Association (PIMA)
1001 Pennsylvania Avenue, NW
Suite 500 North
Washington, DC 20004
E-mail: pima@pima.org
Phone: (202) 624-2709
Fax: (202) 628-3856

Rocky Mountain Institute
1739 Snowmass Creek Road
Snowmass, CO 81654-9199
E-mail: outreach@rmi.org
Phone: (970) 927-3851
Fax: (970) 927-3420

Solar Energy Industries Association (SEIA)
Phone: (703) 248-0702
Fax: (703) 248-0714

Solar Rating and Certification Corporation (SRCC)
C/O FSEC, 1679 Clearlake Road
Cocoa, FL 32922-5703
E-mail: SRCC@FSEC.ucf.edu
Phone: (407) 638-1537
Fax: (407) 638-1010

U.S. Department of Energy's Energy Efficiency and
    Renewable Energy Clearinghouse (EREC)
P.O. Box 3048
Merrifield, VA 22116
E-mail: doe.erec@nciinc.com
Fax: (703) 893-0400
TDD: (800) 273-2957
BBS: (800) 273-2955
(800) DOE-EREC; (800-363-3732)

U.S. Department of Energy's
Office of Building Technology,
State and Community Programs (BTS), EE41
1000 Independence Avenue SW
Washington, DC 20585

References

Association of Home Appliance Manufacturers
1111 19th Street, NW
Suite 402
Washington, DC 20036
(202) 872-5955

Heede, Richard, et al. *Homemade Money*
The Rocky Mountain Institute
1739 Snowmass Creek Road
Snowmass, CO 81654-9199
(970) 927-3851

U.S. Department of Energy's
Energy Efficiency and Renewable
Energy Clearinghouse Fact Sheets
P.O. Box 3048
Merrifield, VA 22116
(800) DOE-EREC; (800-363-3732)

U.S. Department of Energy
Office of Building Technologies,
State and Community Programs
Core Databook, May, 1997

Wilson, Alex, and Morrill, John
Consumer Guide to Home Energy Savings
American Council for an Energy-Efficient
    Economy (ACEEE)
1001 Connecticut Avenue, Suite 801
Washington, D.C. 20036.

References

Available to the public from:

An animated version of *Energy Savers:
Tips on Saving Energy & Money at
Home*
is available online at www.eren.doe.gov/
consumerinfo/energy_savers

National Technical Information Service
(NTIS)
U.S. Department of Commerce
5285 Port Royal Road
Springfield, VA 22161
(703)605-6000 or (800)553-6847
or
DOE Information Bridge
http://www.osti.gov/bridge/

U.S. Department of Energy's Energy
Efficiency
and Renewable Energy Clearinghouse (EREC)
(800)DOE-EREC; (800-363-3732)
E-mail: doe.erec@nciinc.com

Available to DOE and DOE contractors from:

Office of Scientific and Technical
Information (OSTI)

P.O. Box 62
Oak Ridge, TN 37831
(423)576-8401

Energy Savers: Tips on Saving Energy & Money at Home
is available online at www.eren.doe.gov/consumerinfo/energy_savers.

Produced for the
U.S. Department of Energy (DOE)
by the National Renewable Energy Laboratory,
a DOE national laboratory

Funding and technical preparation provided by
DOE's Office of Building Technology, State and
Community Programs, www.eren.doe.gov/build-
ings; Office of Energy Efficiency and Renewable
Energy

DOE/GO-102000-1121
August 2001

Illustrations © 1998 Greening America

GLOSSARY

Aerator

A screened device that is screwed onto the spout of most bathroom and some kitchen faucets to add air into the water and to screen out particulates.

Air Filter

A furnace filter installed in line with the cold air return, which filters out dust and debris and prevents its re-entry into the occupied interior.

Air Return

A furnace duct through which interior air returns to the furnace. The cool air is circulated through the heat exchanger, warmed, and redistributed through the ducts.

Aluminum Wiring

A type of conductor used to carry current. The U.S. Consumer Product Safety Commission has determined that aluminum wiring used in 120 volt light and outlet circuits can be hazardous and a cause of fire. A failure can occur because aluminum wire behaves differently than copper wire when current travels through the conductor. An aluminum wire will expand and contract more than a copper wire. The expansion and contraction can result in loose connections. The loose connections can oxidize. The loose, oxidized connections can spark or overheat when current flows to the connection. The spark or overheating can cause a fire. This potential problem has nothing to do with the wires in the walls, floors, or ceilings. This problem occurs only at the connections. It is possible to control and repair this condition. Typically, aluminum is no longer used in the individual branch lighting and receptacle circuits. It is still commonly used and approved to bring power to a structure and to energize the distribution panels as well as power the individual appliance circuits. Aluminum wire should only be connected to listed and rated devices (breakers, outlets, switches, etc.). Additionally, these devices should have an antioxidant installed to cover the connections.

Amp

Short for Amperes. A measure of the amount of electrical current going through a circuit at any given time.

Angle Stop

A shut-off valve arranged in a 90-degree configuration. It is used to shut off the flow of water to a fixture.

Bearing Wall

A wall that carries the weight or load of the home. Most exterior walls are load bearing along with some interior walls that support the upper floors and or roof.

Blower

A fan in a furnace or air conditioning unit which blows air through ducts.

Boiler

A heating device which heats hot water or creates steam for circulation in heating pipes, radiators, baseboards, or convectors.

Bonnet Nut

The nut in a faucet handle that holds the stem of the faucet, under the handle.

Branch Circuit Panel

The main electrical disconnect for some homes, all power is disconnected with one circuit breaker.

Built-Up Roof

Also called "tar and gravel." The covering is built up from layers of roofing felt, each being sealed with hot tar. Several layers of tar and felt are laid down and covered with a final "flood coat" of hot tar. Small diameter pea-sized gravel is then embedded to protect the underlying layers of felt from sun and weather damage.

Caisson

A truck mounted drill rig drills holes at each corner of the foundation footprint as well as about every 8 feet between the corners, until bedrock is hit. After the holes are drilled, a cage of reinforcing steel is placed into each hole before it is filled with ready-mixed concrete. The resulting columns are called caissons.

Circuit Breaker

An overcurrent protection device which automatically opens an electrical circuit when too much current flows through the conductor.

Cold Joint

A joint in concrete when there is a substantial delay between the placement of layers of concrete. Usually not a problem unless it leaks water or shows displacement.

Compressor

A pump that forces refrigerant through an air conditioning system.

Conduit

A hollow pipe (metal or plastic) casing through which electric wires run.

Cracked Heat Exchanger

A fracture in the walls of the furnace combustion chamber. The heat exchanger separates the flame and combustion products from the air chamber. A crack in the heat exchanger may allow the products of combustion to enter the occupied interior. One of the products of combustion is carbon monoxide. The most common course of action is to replace the furnace.

Current

A flow of electric charge.

Curtain Drain

Similar to a perimeter drain but placed below the footings, about 4 feet away from the foundation. Its purpose is to attract water and intercept it while the water is moving thorough the ground before it reaches the foundation. Popular in retrofit applications.

Daisy Chained

Electrical outlets are connected so that power is supplied from the circuit breaker protecting that specific circuit to the first receptacle on the line, then on to the next, and so forth, until it reaches the last receptacle on the line.

Dead-Front

Switches, circuit breakers, switchboards, control panels and panel board fronts must be covered so that no current-carrying parts are exposed. This cover is called a Dead-Front.

Discharge Standpipe

An open pipe, usually 1½" or 2", mounted in the wall near where the washing machine is, used for the discharge of the used water.

Disposer Wrench

A special tool made to aid in un-jamming disposer blades.

Double-up Branch Circuit

Two circuits controlled by one over current protection device. This wiring method increases the possibility of tripping the over current protection device. Each circuit should be separately fused with an over current protection device of appropriate amperage.

Ducts

Metal piping used for distributing warm or cool air.

Engineered Lumber

Laminates of different woods.

Evaporation Coils

The part of the air conditioning system where the refrigerant returns to gaseous form. Frequently located in the furnace plenum.

Evaporative Cooler

Used in low humidity areas. Outside air is blown into the home through water saturated pads, cooling the air.

Exterior Insulated Finish System, EIFS

Consists of a layer of one-inch think foam insulation board applied over the exterior framing of the dwelling. This layer of foam insulation board is then covered with several layers of acrylic stucco applied over nylon mesh reinforcement. Because the exterior coating is applied over foam insulation, EIFS adds significantly to the overall thermal efficiency of the dwelling and is desirable because of its low maintenance requirement. However, it also can be soft, making it somewhat vulnerable to damage from impact, wood-pecking birds, and carpenter ants.

Finger-Jointed Studs

Made through a process where shorter lengths of wood are glued together and cured into longer lengths. Finger-jointed studs have the same strength as traditional lumber.

Flashing

Material used at connections and penetrations in a roof or wall to prevent leakage.

Flexible Gas Connector

Older installations of gas-fired appliances often use rigid gas piping. This piping is subject to damage in the event of support movement. We recommend that all gas-fired appliances be equipped with flexible gas connectors or swing joints as appropriate. This should also help reduce damage in the event of an earthquake.

Floating Floors

A solution to swelling soils. The basement walls are hung from the floor above and nothing touches the basement floor except the bottom of the stairs, and that is hinged to allow it to rise if the floor rises.

Floor Trusses

A floor truss is wood members fastened together using geometric designs with connector plates to form structures that support a particular floor load.

Forced Air System

A heating system in which air is heated in a furnace and distributed through a structure aided by a blower.

Foundation Drains

A clay or perforated pipe laid around the perimeter of the foundation to collect water and direct it to a sump pump or to a discharge area away from the foundation.

Foundation Vents

Vents along the foundation of a crawl space. Allows moisture from building up in crawl spaces.

French Drains

A pipeless drainage system consisting of a pathway of crushed stone surrounded by fabric up against the foundation wall leading to a gravel filled pit away from the foundation.

Frost Line

The bottom of a frozen layer of soil, several inches to several feet below the surface.

Fuse

An over current protection device with a circuit opening fusible member directly heated and destroyed by the passage of too much current through it.

Gable Roof

A roof with two pitches, designed to provide more space on the upper floors.

Ground Fault Circuit Interrupter, GFCI

Ground Fault Circuit Interrupter: a safety device which monitors the difference between current flowing through the hot and neutral wires of a receptacle. If there is an imbalance of current greater than five milliamps, the current will be cut off in less than a second. GFCI protection is recommended in the garage, outdoor, and bathroom receptacles. We also recommend that all pool and spa equipment have GFCI protection. We further recommend that all kitchen receptacles within six feet of a sink be equipped with GFCI devices. This will reduce shock and short hazards.

Grade

The ground level around a structure. When the ground is less than six inches below the top of the foundation, it is considered a marginal grade. A faulty or marginal grade can lead to moisture damage and/or pest control problems.

Grade Beam on Caisson

Cement beams are poured along the home's footprint, horizontally from caisson to caisson. The beams are made of ready-mix concrete with reinforced steel rods. The beams transfer the weight of the home to the caissons, then to the bedrock.

Grounded

A conducting connection, whether intentional or accidental, between an electrical circuit or equipment and the earth, or to some conducting body that serves in the place of the earth.

The Homeowner's Handbook

Heat Exchanger

A device by which heat is exchanged from one heat-carrying medium to another without direct contact between the two media.

Heat Pump

A central air conditioning system that can run in reverse and transfer heat from outside the home to the inside.

Hip Roof

A roof with no gables; usually has inclined planes on all four sides of the building.

Hose Bibbs

Outside hose faucets.

HVAC Unit

A single unit which supplies heating, venting and air conditioning.

I-Joist

An engineered beam made up of two end caps and a centerpiece. Lighter in weight than dimensional lumber. Named because it looks like a capital "I".

Joist and Rafter Roof

Joists are laid horizontally from bearing wall to bearing wall to provide protection from weather (a flat roof). Eventually humans discovered geometry and raised the joists into triangles, then added rafters to provide slope to a roof.

Joists

Parallel, horizontal boards laid edgewise from wall to wall to support the boards of a floor or ceiling.

Lap Siding

Planking of any suitable material, i.e. wood or aluminum, installed horizontally on the exterior of a home. Often, the bottom of each piece lapped over the outside face of the piece below, allowing water washing down the exterior surface to be directed to the outside face of the cladding.

Main Disconnect

A device by which the electrical system can be disconnected from its source of sup-

ply. Six or more branch circuits require a main disconnect device.

Mastic

Asphalt material used to seal around roof connections and penetrations.

Multi-Wire Branch Circuit

An electrical circuit consisting of two or more ungrounded conductors having a potential difference between them and a grounded conductor having equal potential difference between it and each ungrounded conductor. This type of circuit is commonly used to energize the dishwasher and garbage disposal outlet located in the sink base cabinet. A common problem arises when both hot conductors of the circuit are connected to the same pole or leg of the distribution panel. If both the dishwasher and disposal are operated at the same time, the breaker protecting the circuit will not trip. This is a potential hazard and the circuit should be repaired.

Nail Pops

Drywall nails that work themselves loose and push the drywall mud out slightly.

Negative Grading

Grading which is sloped toward the structure. Low spots and negative grading will increase the chances of water penetration through the foundation, subsequent pooling or puddling in the basement, garage and/or subarea. We recommend that the site be regraded to make sure that surface water runs away from the structure. Any damaged material found in the course of this work should be replaced.

Non-Bearing Wall

A wall that does not carry a load from above. Usually an interior wall that acts as a divider between rooms.

Outlet (Electrical)

A switch, light or receptacle.

Overfused

A fuse or breaker too large for the rated capacity of the circuit. This allows too much current to flow through the conductor (wire) before the overcurrent protection device blows or trips. This is hazardous. The rated capacity of the circuit may not have been exceeded yet. However, increased demand on the circuit may result in the conductor overheating, which can cause a fire. We recommend that all overfused branch circuits be repaired and equipped with overcurrent protection devices of appropriate amperage.

Overhead Wires

Can be a safety hazard. Minimum clearance is 10' in the yard, 12' over a driveway, 18' over a swimming pool and 3' horizontal clearance from a deck or porch.

Overlamping

Putting too high a watt bulb into a socket, i.e. 100 watt bulb into a 60 watt rated lamp,

Partition Wall

Non-weight bearing interior walls.

Perimeter Wall Foundation

A foundation under the entire edge of the home, allows for a crawl space or basement. Is sufficient for a home on stable soils.

Plenum

A large duct or air chamber in which the hot air from the furnace is distributed to the ducting and through the ducts to the registers.

Polarized Plug

One of the blades on the plug is larger than the other so the appliance plug can be inserted into the outlet only one way. This properly aligns hot and neutral wires to reduce the risk of an electric shock.

Post and Beam

A type of construction that utilizes large posts with beams laid horizontally that act as the supports for the roof. Has the advantage of allowing for large areas of windows, because the posts can be spaced far apart.

PVC (Polyvinyl Chloride) Piping

Rigid white plastic pipe and fittings used for supply of domestic water and yard sprin-

kler systems and in interior drain, waste, and vent systems. Introduced in the 1960s.

Radiant Ceiling Heat

Uses electric wires embedded in the ceiling, creating radiant heat. It warms the objects in the room, not the air.

Rafter

One of a series of inclined structural members, which support the roof, running from the exterior wall to the ridge board.

Receptacle

An electrical device to receive the prongs of a plug and which is connected to an electric circuit.

Ridge Vents

Vents installed near the ridge of a roof to allow for removal of excess hot air and to control moisture build up (can be powered or non-powered).

Scuppers

Roof drains.

Slab on Grade

A large block of concrete laid upon the ground. This type of foundation is less expensive than other foundations, but there can be no crawl space or basement beneath it.

Soffit

Decorative covering of open space, usually between kitchen cabinets and the ceiling.

Split-Buss Panels

The main electrical disconnect for some homes. There is a main lighting circuit breaker and other individual circuit breakers. All must be shut off to disconnect all power to the home.

Spread Footing Foundation

Also known as "continuous" foundation. Construction below or partly below grade, which provides support for exterior walls or other structural parts of the building.

Stucco

Comprised of a mixture of sand, water, and Portland cement, which is usually trowel applied over wire reinforcing mesh – called "wire lath" – which has been attached with special "spacer nails" to the exterior substrate of the dwelling.

Sump Pump

A sump cavity located in a corner of the basement or crawlspace for foundation drains to channel water into is drained by a sump pump out and away from the foundation.

Swales

Ditch-like landscape grading that channels water away from foundations and between homes.

Swelling Soils

Contain a lot of clay and can swell when it rains, or snow melts.

Switched Electrical Outlets

An outlet that is connected to a wall switch, allowing a homeowner to turn on a floor lamp that is plugged into the switched half of a duplex plug, by turning on the wall switch.

Temperature Pressure Valve

A safety valve designed to release excess temperature and pressure. Commonly used in water heaters and steam boilers.

Thermostat

An automatic heating/cooling control device. Some units are controlled by clocks to set back the temperature during certain time periods as a fuel-saving measure.

Three-Pronged Plug

On a three-wire cord provides a path for electricity from an electrical product to leave the product.

Three Way Switches

Light switches that have a third wire running between two switches and a light, allowing the light to be turned off and on from two locations.

Tile Roof

Fired clay, stone, or concrete roofing material. Tile roofs are highly resistant to wear and can have a life expectancy of up to fifty plus years.

Valley

A depressed angle formed where two roof planes meet.

Voltage

Electric power. The greater the speed at which electrons travel, the more power present (240 volts is more powerful than 120 volts).

Wall Cladding

Any material used on the exterior walls, it repels moisture, protects the structure and provides a strong, low-maintenance finish.

Washerless Faucet

Most modern faucets now have cartridges instead of washers.

Water Hammer

A sudden pounding noise in a piping system caused by rapid pressure changes due to very quick closing of valves or other restrictions. It is possible to correct this condition by installing an air chamber.

Watt

The amount of electricity flowing through a line, measured in terms of watts. Volts multiplied by amps equals watts.

Weep Screed

The face of a stucco wall extends out an inch or so beyond the underlying foundation. This projection allows any moisture that might penetrate the exterior wall to "weep" out from under the stucco at the bottom.

INDEX

A

Aerator, faucet 36

Air ducts (for furnaces, hot water heaters)
................................64

Air filters (furnace) 61

Aluminum wiring................................50

Anti-siphon device (for hose bibbs) 32

Artificial stucco or EIFS 30

Asphalt composite shingles 26-27

Auxiliary heating device 60

B

Basements, finishing of 11, 16

Blower (furnace) 64

Branch circuit panel 52

Built-up roof................................27

Burners (furnace) 60, 64

C

Caissons 12, 13

Carbon monoxide alarm 57

Cartridges, faucet 37

Cedar shakes 26

Ceiling fans 54-56, 67, 71

Central air conditioning 67-69

    components of 67-69

    whole-house 67, 70

    window units 68

    maintenance of................................67-71

Cinderblock perimeter wall 11

Circuit breaker

    types of 43, 45-49, 52-54

    securing 54

Circuit breaker GFCI 48-49

Circulating pump (furnace) 62, 63

Cladding, wall 29-30

Clay tile (roof) 26-27

Clothes dryer................................76

    venting 76

    maintenance tips 76, 78

Clothes washer, maintenance tips....75-76, 78

Clothes washer water supply hose 75

Conventional hose bibb................................32

Cooling systems, types of................................67-71

Crawl space 13, 19, 20, 22

Concrete floor 15, 16

Cracks................................16, 22, 23

    evaluating seriousness of 22, 23

    shrinkage, treatment for 74

Cut and fill (soil technique)................................19

D

Dimmer switch 55

Doors, rubbing on frames................................72-75

Disposers, troubleshooting 39

Drainage system 20, 21

E

EIFS cladding 30

Electrical service entrance 51, 53

    service drop 51

    service lateral 51

Electrical systems.................................47, 50

Energy Savers, Tips on Saving Energy and
    Money at Home (attachment) 79-113

Engineered lumber 15

Evaporative coolers 67, 69

Expanding soils 11, 12

Expansion tank 62, 63

Exterior hose bibbs

    description 32

    shutting down for winter.......................32

Exterior Insulated Finish System 30

Exterior moisture, effects of 20

Exterior outlets (electrical) 54-55

F

Factory-fabricated trusses.....................15, 18

Faucet washer 36

Faucets, washerless 37

Flashing, roof...25, 28

Flat or low-sloped roofs 26-27

Floated floor 16

Floor-mounted outlets (electrical) 55

Floor system 15, 16

Floor trusses 15

Floors, squeaks 75

Flush valve, toilet 38

Foam board insulation 30

Footing, foundation 11, 12

Forced-air heating system 59, 60-61

Foundation, types 8-16, 19-23

Foundation's footprint 11

Freeze-proof hose bibb 32

French drain 21

Frost line 11

Fuel-fired heating systems 64

Furnace filter 60-61

Furnaces, types of 60, 62-64

G

Garage door openers 31, 33

Gas-fueled boiler (furnance) 62

GFCI receptacles 45-46

Glossary 114-119

Grade beam on caisson 12, 13

Grade beam on drilled pier 12

Gravel built-up roof.....................................27

Ground-fault circuit-interrupters,
    types of 45-49, 54

H

Hammock filter (furnace)................................61

Heat exchanger (furnace) 60-61

Heat pump (furnace) 59-61

Horizontal outlets (electrical) 55-55

Hose bibbs 32

Hose faucets 25, 32

Hot water heating systems......................62-63

Humidifiers 61

I

Inlet valve, toilet 38

I-joist 15

J

Joist and rafter roof 18

L

Load-bearing wall 10, 14

Lumber-framed bearing wall 17

M

Main disconnect......................................51-54

Main distribution panel (electrical) 52

Masonry wall 29

Moisture, effects on home, siding 29

Moisture

exterior 8-9, 11, 19-21, 23

interior 77

N

Nail pops, treatment for................................74

Non-bearing wall 17

Non-freeze-proof hose bibb 32

O

Oriented strand board (OSB) siding 29

P

Partition wall 17

Perimeter wall foundation 11-13

Portable GFCI...46

Post and beam walls....................................17

Propane gas alarm 57

R

Radiant ceiling heating systems 65

Radon gas...64

Reinforcing cable, materials 14

Roof, extending life of................................28

Roof flashing 28

Roofs 24-28

sloped 26-27

flat or low-sloped................................26-27

S

Seasonal home maintenance tasks..............78

Settlement, soil 19

Shrinkage cracks 74

Siding, types of...29-30

Single-throw switch 55

Slab-on-grade foundation 13-15

Slate roofs 27

Sloped roofs 26-27

Smoke alarm 57

Split-buss panel (electrical)........................53

Spread-footing foundation 11-12

Sprinkler system,
    when and how to shut down 25,33

Squeaking floors 75

Stable soil...12, 19

Stucco 29-30

Sump cavity 21

SureVoid® 13

Swale 20-21

Swelling soil.................................12, 16, 19

Switched electrical outlets 54-55

T

Tar and gravel roof covering.......................27

Thermostat (furnace) 60, 62-63

3-way switched lights or 3-way circuit
   54-55

Toilets, components of................................38

U

Underlayment, roof.......................................26

Unstable soil 12-13

V

Ventilation 77

W

Wall cladding 29-30

Wall receptacle type GFCI.......................45-46

Walls, types of 24-25, 29

Water Heaters..40-41

Water ponding (on roof) 27

Washerless faucets 37

Water supply hose (clothes washer) 75

Watertight membrane (for no-slope roofs)
   27

Weather shell 24-25

Weep screed 29-30

Whole-house fans................................67, 70-71

Wires 43-49, 50

    overhead 44

    minimum clearances 44

Wood and wood-composite siding 29

Wood-framed floors 15

Wood shingles 26

The Homeowner's Handbook

The Homeowner's Handbook